No Island Is an Island

ITALIAN ACADEMY LECTURE SERIES

The
Italian
Academy

ITALIAN ACADEMY LECTURES

Umberto Eco,
Serendipities: Language and Lunacy

No Island Is an Island

FOUR GLANCES AT ENGLISH LITERATURE IN A WORLD PERSPECTIVE

Carlo Ginzburg

Introduction translated by John Tedeschi

Columbia University Press
New York

Columbia University Press
Publishers Since 1893
New York   Chichester, West Sussex

Copyright © 2000 Columbia University Press
All rights reserved

Library of Congress Cataloging-in-Publication Data
Ginzburg, Carlo.
    No island is an island : four glances at English literature in a world
perspective / Carlo Ginzburg ; introduction translated by John Tedeschi.
        p.   cm. — (Italian academy lectures)
    Includes bibliographical references and index.
    Contents: The old world and the new seen from nowhere — Selfhood as
otherness : constructing English identity in the Elizabethan age — A search
for origins : rereading Tristram Shandy — Tusitala and his Polish reader.
    ISBN 0-231-11628-4 (alk. paper)
        1. English literature—History and criticism. 2. English literature—Early
modern, 1500–1700—History and criticism. 3. Sterne, Laurence, 1713–1768.
Life and opinions of Tristram Shandy, gentleman. 4. More, Thomas, Sir,
Saint, 1478–1535. Utopia. 5. Stevenson, Robert Louis, 1850–1894—Influence.
6. Difference (Psychology) in literature. 7. Identity (Psychology) in literature.
8. Malinowski, Bronislaw, 1884–1942. 9. Literature and anthropology.
10. Utopias. I. Title. II. Series.

PR99.G516 2000
820.9'353—dc21

00-035844

Casebound editions of Columbia University Press books
are printed on permanent and durable acid-free paper.
Printed in the United States of America
Designed by Linda Secondari
c 10 9 8 7 6 5 4 3 2 1

Contents

List of Illustrations

Acknowledgments

THE FOUR ESSAYS THAT FOLLOW were presented before the Italian Academy of New York in February and March 1998. I should like to thank Richard Brilliant for the opportunity to spend two delightful months of research at the Casa Italiana, of which he is the director.

The themes discussed in this small book were the subject, in a slightly different form, of the Clark Lectures delivered at Cambridge in January 1998. I am grateful to Amartya Sen and Emma Rothschild for their warm hospitality at Trinity College.

Many people have helped me in a variety of ways, both in Cambridge and New York. It is impossible to thank them all. I shall mention only one, Franco Moretti, with whom, during long walks and late evening conversations, I continued a dialogue that has endured over many years.

I am very grateful to my friend John Tedeschi for having translated my introduction, to Sam Gilbert for his thorough stylistic revision, and to Sarah St. Onge for her very competent editing, which much improved my text.

Introduction

THESE FOUR ESSAYS PROPOSING a noninsular vision of English literature are connected by a common theme: the island, both real and
imagined, evoked in the title. But the unity of the book is not only (and
perhaps not even principally) of a thematic order. A similar construc-
tive principle has guided my researches and the ways in which I presented them, although it is only in retrospect that I am able to identify some of these characteristics.

It always began with a discovery originating on the fringe of a wholly different investigation. It was chance, not deliberate curiosity, that
made me stumble on Bishop Vasco de Quiroga's reactions to Thomas
More's *Utopia*, or on Samuel Daniel's *Defence of Ryme*, and so forth. On
each occasion I felt the sudden sensation that I had come upon something, perhaps even something important; at the same time I felt an
acute awareness of ignorance. Sometimes an answer flashed before me:
for example, the perception of a morphological affinity between *Tristram
Shandy* and Bayle's *Dictionnaire*. But what was the question? Only research
permitted me eventually to formulate it. I do not know if beginning at
the end, at the solution, and proceeding backward is the way others
usually practice intellectual work. I have the impression that in my case
this propensity has become more pronounced along the way, for reasons that are both objective and subjective.

Let me begin with the former, which is tied to the limitations of the essay, a literary genre that I have practiced almost exclusively in the last decade. In "The Essay as Form," Adorno writes: "The essay becomes true in its progress. . . . Its concepts receive their light from a *terminus ad quem* hidden to the essay itself, and not from an obvious *terminus a quo*."[1]

Here and elsewhere Adorno is emphasizing the nondeductive element proper to the essay as a genre. For a person reading an essay, the end results, the *terminus ad quem* of a generally tortuous course, are by definition unknown, hence the surprise accompanying the reading of the best examples of this literary form. For the writer, however, the final destination is known, often before he or she begins to write. To suppose that it may even be known before starting the research means greatly increasing the possibilities offered by the formal characteristics of the essay. This is what I think I have done, even if not deliberately.

But are these really essays that I am presenting here? Anyone familiar with the tradition, preeminently English, inaugurated by Addison and Lamb—urbane and cosmopolitan conversation, elegantly informal, on themes that are often simply pretexts—will deny the attribute of essays to these pages that have so little of the light-hearted about them and are weighed down by erudite observations. But those who identify the essay as a genre progressing from Montaigne to Diderot and beyond will not be frightened by notes. Erudition dominates the convivial discussions in which the remote origins of the essay as a literary form can be identified.[2] And the very etymology of the word "essay" (from the Low Latin *exagium*, "balance") associates the genre, as Jean Starobinski has reminded us, with the need to submit ideas for verification.[3] But the term always oscillates between "test" and "endeavor," as in the famous passage from Montaigne: "En fin, toute cette fricassée que je barbouille icy n'est qu'un registre des essais de ma vie" (*Essais* 3:13).[4] This is an eloquent ambiguity, even if not an isolated one: it suffices to think of the Italian *prova* (proof, test). No verification can be considered definitive:

speaking of the essay, Adorno cautions, "self-relativization is immanent in its form."[5]

The tortuous, capricious, discontinuous progression of the essay appears to be incompatible with the rigor of the test. But perhaps this flexibility is precisely what succeeds in capturing configurations that tend to elude the grasp of the institutional disciplines. The divergence between Quentin Skinner and myself regarding the genre to which More's *Utopia* belongs may be instructive (see chapter 1). Someone could object that the *Utopia* constitutes a special case, since it is one of those rare texts that inaugurated a literary genre. But I ask myself how an apparently technical controversy such as the one over the legitimacy of the rhyme that flared up in Elizabethan England could have been misinterpreted to the point of ignoring its continental roots, beginning with Montaigne (see chapter 2). Cases of this sort can easily be found. In the game of chess that is research the majestic literary rooks move implacably in a straight line; the essay as a genre instead moves like the knight in an unforeseeable manner, jumping from one discipline to another, from one textual entity to another.[6]

But subjective predilections as well have entered in the construction of the inquiries contained in this volume. Twenty years ago, in an essay entitled "Clues," I suggested a hypothesis, "obviously unverifiable," explaining the origin of the narrative that has aroused the interest of a number of literary scholars such as Terence Cave, Christopher Prendergast, and Antoine Compagnon. The very idea of narration, I conjectured at the time, could have arisen in a society of hunters, for the purpose of transmitting on the basis of infinitesimal traces an event that could not be directly experienced, an acknowledgment that "someone passed this way." With this model taken from the chase (or, if projected into the future, from divination), which I dubbed an "evidential paradigm," I was trying to give some direction to my way of conducting research by introducing it into an exceedingly distant historical perspective, indeed a plurimillenarian one.[7] I dwell on that essay, which from that time has continued to sustain my research subterraneously, because the hypothesis on the origin of narrative formulated at that time can shed light also on historical narrative: dedicated, unlike other forms, to the search for truth and thus shaped, in every phase, by questions and answers in narrative form.[8] To read reality backward, starting from its opacity, so as to avoid remaining prisoners of the designs of the intellect: this notion dear to Proust, it seems to me, expresses an ideal of research that has also inspired the following pages.[9]

I began working as a historian examining nonliterary texts (especially Inquisitorial trials) with the aid of interpretative tools developed by such scholars as Leo Spitzer, Erich Auerbach, and Gianfranco Contini.[10] It was probably inevitable that sooner or later I should end up occupying myself also with literary texts. But this new research experience has taken into account lessons learned in the past. From the Friulian miller Domenico Scandella, nicknamed Menocchio, condemned to death by the Inquisition for his ideas, I grasped that the way in which a human being appropriates his or her readings is frequently unpredictable.[11] I approach, with a similar perspective, Vasco de Quiroga, reader of Lucian and of Thomas More; Thomas More, reader of Lucian; George Puttenham and Samuel Daniel, readers of Montaigne; Sterne, reader of Bayle; and so forth. In each of these cases I have attempted to analyze not the reworking of a source but something broader and more fleeting: the relationship of reading with writing, of the present with the past with the present.

No Island Is an Island

CHAPTER ONE

The Old World and the New
Seen from Nowhere

1

SUCCESS CAN BE A BLINDING FORCE. The enormous impact of Thomas More's *Utopia* has inspired many attempts by its interpreters to place the book in its historical context. But the more or less convincing alternatives that have polarized the scholarly debate for a long time—Middle Ages versus Renaissance, jeu d'esprit versus serious political reflection, and so forth—have usually failed to take into account the multiple dimensions of a text that is often regarded as strangely elusive.

Quentin Skinner's authoritative essay permits us to begin with a different focus. He starts from "the general subject matter of the book," announced "on the title page, which reads: *De optimo reipublicae statu deque nova insula Utopia*. [More's] concern, that is, is not merely or even primarily with the new island of Utopia; it is with 'the best state of a commonwealth.' " Having clarified this, Skinner suggests "a way of approaching the complexities of More's text. If *Utopia* is an instance of a familiar genre of Renaissance political theory, it may be best to begin not with More's text itself but rather with some attempt to indicate the assumptions and conventions characteristic of the genre as a whole."

Skinner argues that several passages of More's *Utopia* are either echoes of, or allusions to, texts widely read by humanists that were related to the discussion on the best state of a commonwealth, such as Cicero's *De officiis*. According to Skinner, More demonstrates that "if vir-

tue constitutes the only true nobility, it may be incoherent simply to en-
dorse the usual justification for private property."[1] Likewise, Plato's arguments for abolishing private property would have shown the incon-
sistency of the humanist tradition, which was based on Cicero.

The presence of echoes of Cicero and Plato in More's *Utopia* is unde-
niable, but Skinner's general argument seems unconvincing. On a theoretical level, I am certainly sympathetic with Skinner's emphasis on a
contextual approach to the texts of the past. But does More's *Utopia* be-
long wholly, as Skinner suggests, to the genre of Renaissance political
theory dealing with the best state of a commonwealth? Skinner starts
his contextualizing strategy with *Utopia*'s title, but his quotation is curi-
ously incomplete. The full title of the first edition, published in Louvain
by Dierk Martens toward the end of 1516, is *Libellus vere aureus nec minus
salutaris quam festivus de optimo reipublicae statu, deque nova insula Utopia* [A truly
golden handbook, no less beneficial than entertaining, on the best state
of a commonwealth and the new island of Utopia].

In the second edition, issued in Paris in 1517, the words "nec minus
salutaris quam festivus" became "non minus utile quam elegans." The
third edition returned to the original text. The word *festivus*—I will trans-
late it for the moment as "playful, entertaining"—seems rather inappropriate to the austere tradition of political philosophy in which, according to Skinner, *Utopia* should be placed. The book, I will argue, is a tree
from a different forest. The two adjectives "nec minus salutaris quam
festivus," "no less beneficial than entertaining," as well as their relationship, seem to point to a different tradition.[2]

In emphasizing the importance of a word like *festivus* I may seem to
be following C. S. Lewis's well-known advice not to take More's book *au
grand sérieux*, as modern readers have tended to do.[3] On the contrary, I
believe that the serious, sometimes chilling side of More's *Utopia* is absolutely crucial if we are to understand the book's general meaning. But
if my conclusion is bound to diverge from C. S. Lewis's, the path I will

follow is close to the one he suggested a long time ago. I will also, like many others, start from the letters and documents, written either by Thomas More or by his friends and acquaintances, that were included in the early editions of *Utopia*.[4]

2

The first publication of *Utopia* was closely supervised by Erasmus. Through his letters we can follow, nearly day by day, how he collected, and presumably polished, introductory letters, added marginal notes, and praised the book to prominent humanists such as Guillaume Budé, who later contributed a long letter to the second edition.[5] I will come back later to the significance of Erasmus's intimate involvement in the project. For now, let us begin with the first edition of *Utopia*, the small quarto published in Louvain in 1516.[6]

The reverse of the title page shows a rough map of Utopia, under the title *Utopiae Insulae Figura* (fig. 1.1). The next page displays the Utopian alphabet, a poem in the Utopian language, and its Latin translation (fig. 1.2). Another poem in Utopian follows, "Six lines on the island of Utopia by Anemolius, poet laureate, nephew of Hythlodaeus by his sister," Hythlodaeus being the traveler whose description of the laws and customs of the island fills the second book of More's *Utopia*. Here is the prose translation of that little poem: "The ancients called me Utopia or Nowhere because of my isolation. At present, however, I am a rival of Plato's republic, perhaps even a victor over it. The reason is that what he has delineated [*deliniavit*] in words alone I have displayed [*praestiti*] in men and resources and laws of surpassing excellence. Deservedly ought I to be called by the name of Eutopia or Happy Land."

Deliniavit . . . praestiti: Plato's republic is vanquished by More's Utopia, as a pictorial description is vanquished by the display of the real thing. But is not More's Utopia also a description? Yes, but a description that gives one the feeling of being there. The next item in the first edition, a

FIGURE 1.1. The reverse of the title page of the 1516 Louvain edition of
Utopia, showing a rough map of Utopia, under the title *Utopiae Insulae Figura*.

letter addressed by Peter Giles, chief secretary to the city of Antwerp, to Jerome Busleyden, provost of the church of Aire, made this point emphatically: "A man of great eloquence has represented, painted, and set it before our eyes in such a way that, as often as I read it; I think I see far more than when, being as much a part of the conversation as More himself, I heard Raphael Hythlodaeus's own words sounding in my ears. . . . When I contemplate this same picture painted by More's brush [*Mori penicillo depicta*], I am sometimes as affected as if I were sometimes actually living in Utopia itself."[7]

"Set it before our eyes," *sic oculis subiectam*: this was, according to Greek rhetorical tradition, the aim of *ekphrasis*. Through a description full of what the Greeks, the Romans, and we would have called, respectively, *enargeia*, *evidentia in narratione*, and vividness, absent things—usually works of art, either real or fictitious—or past events were to be evoked, giving the reader an uncanny feeling of reality.[8] Giles, a humanist deeply versed in Greek and Latin, praised More's book as an accomplished instance of *ekphrasis*. But the effect of reality achieved by More's eloquence is reinforced by the provision of documentary evidence directly from the island of Utopia. Giles informs Busleyden (and the reader) that the little poem in Utopian had been handed to him by Raphael Hythlodaeus himself, "after More's departure."

"As to More's uncertainty," he added,

about the geographical position of the island, Raphael had not failed to mention that, but in very few words and as it were in passing, as if reserving the topic for another place. But, somehow or other, an unlucky accident caused us both to fail to catch what he said. While Raphael was speaking on the topic, one of More's servants had come up to him to whisper something or other in his ear. I was therefore listening all the more intently when one of our company who had, I suppose, caught cold on shipboard, coughed a b c d e f g h i k l m n o p q r s t u x y

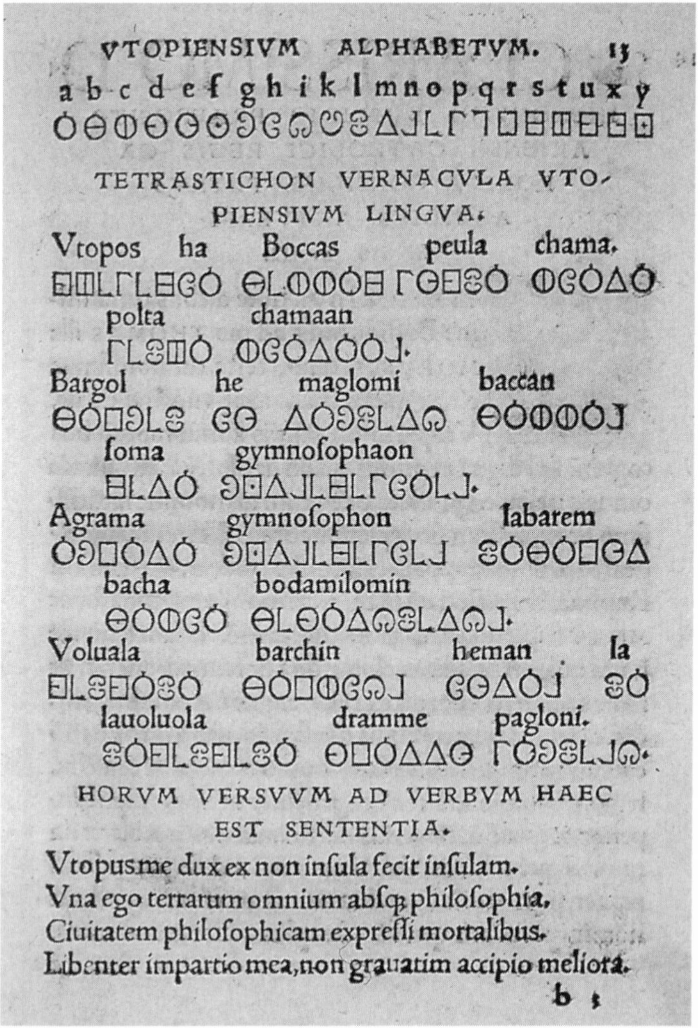

Ȯ ⊖ ⵔ ⵔ ⊖ ⵔ ⵔ ⵔ ⵔ ⵔ ⵔ Δ ⅃ Γ ⅂ ⵔ Β ⵔ ⵔ ⵔ ⵔ

TETRASTICHON VERNACVLA VTO-
PIENSIVM LINGVA.

Vtopos	ha	Boccas	peula	chama.

polta   chamaan

Bargol   he   maglomi   baccan

foma   gymnofophaon

Agrama   gymnofophon   labarem

bacha   bodamilomin

Voluala   barchin   heman   la

lauoluola   dramme   pagloni.

HORVM VERSVVM AD VERBVM HAEC
EST SENTENTIA.

Vtopus me dux ex non infula fecit infulam.
Vna ego terrarum omnium abfq; philofophia,
Ciuitatem philofophicam expreffi mortalibus.
Libenter impartio mea, non grauatim accipio meliora.

b

FIGURE 1.2. The Utopian alphabet, a poem in the Utopian language,
and its Latin translation.

so loudly that I could not make out some phrases of what Raphael said. I shall not rest, however, till I have full information on this point so that I shall be able to tell you exactly not only the location of the island but even the exact distance from the pole—provided that our friend Hythlodaeus be alive and safe.[9]

This passage has often been regarded as a mere joke, but it deserves a closer look, as do the letters, poems, maps, and alphabets that frame More's *Utopia*. What is the relationship between those *paratextes*—as Gérard Genette, the French critic, would call them—and the text itself?[10]

I deliberately said "frame More's *Utopia*." I would compare the coughing witness to the trompe l'oeil fly depicted by Petrus Christus on the painted frame of his wonderful *Portrait of a Carthusian* (fig. 1.3).

In both cases, a trivial, minuscule detail, represented with the greatest possible verisimilitude, is placed on the very threshold of an image—the one painted "by More's brush" (*Mori penicillo depicta*), and the other by Petrus Christus's—in order to tease the beholder. More may have seen a painting like this during his stay in Flanders, where he started to think about his *Utopia*. Presumably he was also familiar with a passage from Philostratus's *Imagines* that, as Panofsky convincingly suggested, may have inspired Petrus Christus: a painter "enamored of verisimilitude" was said by Philostratus to have depicted "a bee settling on the flowers" with such accuracy that it was impossible to say whether "an actual bee had been deceived by the picture or a painted bee deceived the beholder."[11]

The deception game played by More and his friends implied therefore a double move. On the one hand, they scattered their texts with vivid details meant to certify their truthfulness; on the other, they suggested in manifold ways that the whole narrative was fictitious. This self-refutation was conveyed by intricate strategies. Two examples follow.

Here is More, dedicating his *Utopia* to Giles:

FIGURE 1.3. Petrus Christus, *Portrait of a Carthusian*, ca. 1446, Metropolitan Museum of Art, New York.

According to my own recollection, Hythlodaeus declared that the bridge which spans the river Anydrus at Amaurotum is five hundred paces in length. But my John says that two hundred must be taken off, for the river there is not more than three hundred paces in breadth. Please recall the matter to mind. If you agree with him, I shall adopt the same view and think myself mistaken. If you do not remember, I shall put down, as I have actually done, what I myself seem to remember. Just as I shall take great pains to have nothing incorrect in the book, so, if there is doubt about anything, I shall rather tell an objective falsehood than an intentional lie—for I would rather be honest than wise.[12]

The last remark, echoing a passage by Aulus Gellius, elicited an ironical gloss from Erasmus: "Notice the theological distinction between lying and speaking an untruth" (*Nota theologicam differentiam inter mentiri et mendacium dicere*).[13]

Trompe l'oeil always implies a *clin d'oeil*, a wink. To shift from one level to another was clearly a source of real delight for More and Erasmus, and for their audience as well—with some exceptions. Obviously, the game of deceptions was amusing because not everybody got it. The "devout man, a theologian by profession, burning with an extraordinary desire to visit Utopia" and become its bishop, was presumably More's invention. But the fat man who, as Beatus Rhenanus informed Willibald Pirckheimer on February 23, 1518, thought that More had merely transcribed Hythlodaeus's accounts, appeared so ridiculous because he was, or was thought to be, a real person.[14] In a letter addressed to Peter Giles, included as an appendix to *Utopia*'s second edition, More unveiled, in a characteristically devious way, the purpose of his game as well as the boundaries between insiders and outsiders.

"An unusually sharp person," More wrote, "put this dilemma about our *Utopia*: If the facts are reported as true, I see some rather absurd elements in them, but if as fictitious, then I find More's finished judgment wanting in some matters." Now, More retorts, when this fellow "doubts whether Utopia is real or fictitious, then I find his finished judgment wanting." But why should the issue not be open to doubt? The explanation is contained in a few sentences describing some hypothetical possibilities and cast in the subjunctive mood, that is, denoting what More had refrained from doing: "If I had determined to write about the commonwealth [*si de republica scribere decrevissem*] and such a myth [*fabula*] had come to mind, I would perhaps not have shrunk from that fiction whereby the truth, as if smeared with honey, might have slid a little more pleasantly into men's minds. But I should certainly have tempered the fiction so that, even in abusing the ignorance of common folk, I should have included indications permitting at least the more learned to see through our purpose."

But wait. "If I had determined to write about the commonwealth": had not More indeed written a book about the commonwealth, bearing the title *De optimo reipublicae statu*? Once again, More is playfully deceiving his readers. This time he does it by telling them, through a hypothetical sentence implying something unreal, the plain truth: not only what he did, but what he meant to do.[15] He goes on: "Thus, if I had done nothing else than impose such names on ruler, river, city, and island as might suggest to the more learned that the island was nowhere, the city a phantom, the river without water, and the ruler without a people, it would not have been hard to do and would have been much wittier than what I actually did. Had I not been bound by a fidelity to history, I am not so stupid as to have preferred to use such barbarous and meaningless names as Utopia, Anydrus, Amaurotum, and Ademus."[16]

Most scholars have unaccountably overlooked these words, possibly because More's second letter to Giles was not included, until very recently, in later editions of *Utopia*.[17] Gerhard Vossius, the seventeenth-century erudite, even wrote to Samuel Sorbière to communicate the meaning of Utopian names, apparently unaware that he had been anticipated by More himself.[18] Currently and more importantly, the debate about More's allegedly mysterious intentions does not seem to have taken into account the aforementioned passage. If we substitute for the hypothetical the indicative mood, More's intentions are indeed clear: he had planned to write about the commonwealth; a story, or perhaps a myth (*fabula*) occurred to him; he decided to use it in order to make the truth he wished to convey more palatable to his audience. Although he wanted to take advantage of the ignorance of common people, he gave some tongue-in-cheek hints to the *litteratiores*, the intellectual elite, in order to stress the fictitious character of his narrative. A basic knowledge of Greek revealed to those *litteratiores* the paradoxical content of all the names related to (and including) Utopia, beginning with the source of all information, Hythlodaeus, that "expert in nonsense."[19] A minuscule detail proves that More's game depended on the use of Greek. In the first edition he had alluded to the Utopian senate by the phrase "*in senatu Mentirano*," inadvertently employing the Latin term *mentiri*, "to lie"; in later editions he wrote "*in senatu Amaurotico*."[20]

So much for More's explicit intentions. But the meaning of his book is of course another, more complicated matter.[21] The questions to be asked are: Why did More choose to declare his intentions in such a convoluted way? Was the deception game played by More and his friends a mere literary device, or was it something more serious?

The second question has been asked before; even the beginning of my answer will have a familiar ring. In order to understand the meaning of More's *Utopia*, we must reinsert it in a literary tradition initiated by Lucian of Samosata.

3

Recognition of the Lucianic character of Erasmus's *Praise of Folly* (*Encomium Moriae*), which was dedicated to More, as well as of More's *Utopia*, the publication of which Erasmus closely supervised, is now common-place,[22] but it deserves closer scrutiny. Let us start with the collection of Lucian's writings translated by Erasmus and More in 1505 or, more precisely, from the title of the first edition, issued in Paris the following year: *Luciani viri quam disertissimi complurima opuscula longe festivissima*. These *opuscula festivissima* were republished nine times before More's death.[23] Among those later editions, the one published in Florence by the heirs of Filippo Giunta in 1519 is particularly relevant: besides Lucian's writings, it included More's *Utopia*, in Latin. As Carlo Dionisotti pointed out in a remarkable essay, we can safely assume that Machiavelli read this volume attentively.[24] I will consider this edition from a different angle: as a context, in the most literal sense of the word, for *Utopia*'s text.

From 1530 onward, "Lucian" was to many people all over Europe (including John Calvin) a synonym for unbeliever, atheist.[25] So what had Lucian meant to Erasmus and More a few decades earlier? An answer is provided by the prefaces attached to most of the two friends' translations of Lucian's writings. (Incidentally, the addressees of those prefaces included Johannes Paludanus and Jerome Busleyden, who were later involved in the publication of More's *Utopia*.) In his preface to *Alexander, seu pseudomantis* Erasmus wrote that nobody was as useful (*nemo sit utilior*) as Lucian for exposing the lies of those who take advantage of the common people by means either of magical arts or of superstition, meaning of course ecclesiastical superstition. But besides being useful, Erasmus went on, Lucian was also pleasing and therefore suited perfectly the character of René d'Illiers, bishop of Chartres, to whom the translation was dedicated: "Your Excellency is perfectly instructed in those studies which are grave and austere by nature, nevertheless with your gay wit and extremely affable manners [*propter summam ingenii festivitatem, miramque morum iucunditatem*] you do not altogether shun even the more elegant arts such as this, and are in the habit of admitting some frivolous interludes of this useful sort among exacting public duties."[26]

Utilis, festivus, elegans: the adjectives used by Erasmus in this rather perfunctory text reappear in the titles of *Utopia*'s early editions. This cluster of words conveyed a set of values shared by Erasmus and More. They both regarded Lucian as the most accomplished (*elegans*) exemplar of the advice, given by Horace, to mingle *utile dulci* (usefulness and sweetness) and usefulness and playfulness (*festivitas*).[27] Playfulness could therefore become a mask concealing a superior truth, as Cicero said of the use of irony by Socrates: "Socrates was fascinating and witty, a genial conversationalist; he was what the Greeks call εἴρων, in every conversation, pretending to need information and professing admiration for the wisdom of his companion" (*dulcem et facetum festivique sermonis atque in omni oratione simulatorem, quem* εἴρωνα *Graeci nominarunt, Socratem accepimus*) (*De officiis*, I, 30, 108).[28] Erasmus, who was so deeply captivated by Socrates, found the same ironic virtues in More, "that dearest friend, with whom I love to mix up serious things and jokes" (*quicum libenter soleo seria ludicraque miscere*) as well as in Lucian, who "in the same way mixes up serious things with jokes, jokes with serious things" (*sic seria nugis, nugas seriis miscet*).[29]

"I would perhaps not have shrunk from that fiction," More ambiguously declared in his second letter to Peter Giles, "whereby the truth, as if smeared with honey, might have slid a little more pleasantly into men's minds." The pleasant, playful Lucianic connotations of More's *Utopia*, that *Libellus vere aureus nec minus salutaris quam festivus*, thus become clear. But *festivus* had another meaning as well, which did not refer to the form of the book but to its content, not only to the honey, we could say, but to the truth behind it. This other meaning also points to Lucian.

4

The primary meaning of *festivus* is of course related to *festum*, festivity, holiday. In his preface to *Toxaris, de amicitia*, dated London, January 1, 1506, the first dialogue in the aforementioned collection of Lucian's writings, Erasmus addressed himself to Richard Foxe, the founder of Corpus

Christi, in the following terms: "There is a custom which has been handed down from the ages of antiquity to our own times, my lord Bishop,
of sending little presents on the calends of January, the first day of the
New Year. Such presents are thought to bring some kind of good luck
both to the recipients and also to those donors who receive an answering gift." He had looked, Erasmus went on, through his belongings,
but "found nothing among my possessions save poor sheets of paper. I
was obliged, therefore, to send a paper present," that is, the translation
of Lucian's dialogue.[30]

Allen, referring to this text, suggested that the first publication of
More's *Utopia*, toward the end of December 1516, could also have come
about "with a view to its use as a *strena*."[31] It seems to me that More
might have been inspired by the recent publication of a new edition of
Lucian's *Opuscula*, issued in Paris in June 1514, which included three additional, related pieces translated by Erasmus: *Saturnalia*, *Cronosolon, id est
Saturnalium legum lator*, and *Epistolae Saturnales*. In a revised version of his
dedicatory letter to William Warham, which came too late to be included in the Paris edition, Erasmus compared Lucian's *Saturnalia* to a "liter-
aria strenula," a small literary New Year present, "a witty enough book if
I am not mistaken [*libellum nisi fallor nec infestivum*] nor have I hitherto in-
scribed it to any other person; and it will serve your purpose very well,
if ever you have a mind, I should say a moment, to laugh."[32] In these
three related pieces Lucian's irony focused on social inequality:

"Why are you looking so downhearted, Cronosolon?" Cronus asks
the priest.

"Haven't I every reason, master," Cronosolon, the priest, answers,
"when I see disgusting and filthy rogues unbelievably rich leading a
comfortable life, while I and many another educated man know pover-
ty and despair as companions?"

To this sad situation Lucian opposes on the one hand the Golden Age,
Cronus's mythical kingdom, and on the other its ritual counterpart, the

weeklong festival in which social hierarchies were subverted and the slaves were served by their masters. (Since the Romans had identified Cronus with Saturn, the ancient Italic god, the festival was known in Rome as Saturnalia, the title chosen by Erasmus for his translation of Lucian's three pieces). Lucian stresses the egalitarian features of Cronus's festival, as well as its symbolic and ephemeral quality. "This rule of mine," Cronus explains, "doesn't extend beyond dicing, hand-clapping, singing, and getting drunk, and then it's only for seven days. So, regarding the more important matters you mention—removing inequality and all being poor or rich together—Zeus might be willing to deal with them."[33]

In his *Utopia* More dealt precisely with those important matters: "removing inequality and all being poor or rich together." More's *Libellus* was indeed *festivus*, also because it was presumably conceived as a *strena*, a present related to a holiday that in antiquity had subversive (albeit largely symbolic) associations. A learned and perceptive reader like Guillaume Budé did not miss the Saturnian features of More's *Utopia*. In endorsing More's argument that the disappearance of greed would create a much better society, Budé wrote: "Beyond the shadow of a doubt, greed, the vice that perverts and ruins so many minds otherwise extraordinary and lofty, would depart hence once for all, and the golden age of Saturn would return [*et aureum saeculum Saturniumque rediret*]."

One could object that Budé was simply echoing Virgil's famous words *redeunt Saturnia regna* (*Ecloga IV, 6*). But Budé also detected the Lucianic inspiration of More's book as a whole: "Utopia," he wrote, "lies outside the limits of the known world. Undoubtedly it is one of the Fortunate Isles, perhaps close to the Elysian Fields, for More himself testifies that Hythlodaeus has not yet stated its position."[34]

The description of the Elysian Fields forms the core of the second part of Lucian's *True Histories*, a narrative describing a journey into a multitude of strange worlds. Among the famous men inhabiting the Elysian Fields Lucian names various philosophers, such as the followers of

Socrates and Epicurus. Then he ironically remarks: "Plato alone was not there; it was said that he was living in his imaginary city under the constitution and the laws that he himself had written. . . . All of their wives are kept in common. . . . In this point they [the inhabitants of the Elysian fields] out-Plato Plato and give boys to those who wish them without raising any objection."[35]

More's *Utopia* was explicitly indebted to Plato's *Republic* but was also, as Peter Giles remarked, "plus quam platonicam," more than Platonic, and his Plato was filtered through Lucian as well. This is only one of the many paradoxes of More's paradoxical book. In the aforementioned letter to Giles, included in the second edition of his book, More wrote that he had used those "barbarous and meaningless" Utopian names (whose meaning he had in fact just unveiled) because he felt an obligation toward "fidelity to history" (*fides . . . historiae*). In this ironical claim framed by a lie, the *litteratiores*, the learned elite, might have detected once again an allusion to a work of Lucian, in this case the *True Histories*. Lucian had begun by explaining that he was a liar, but one whose lying was far more honest than the miracles and fables written by poets, historians, and philosophers, "for though I tell the truth in nothing else, I shall at least be truthful in saying that I am a liar." Like his Utopians, More was obviously "captivated by the wit and pleasantry of Lucian,"[36] but undoubtedly fascinated also by Lucian's ability to combine the whimsical and the serious, which Erasmus had praised in such eloquent terms: "By his mixture of fun and gravity, gaiety and accurate observation, he effectively portrays the manners, emotions, and pursuits of men, as through a painter's vivid brush, inviting us not so much to read about them as to see them with our own eyes."[37]

5

It has been variously suggested that the entirety of More's *Utopia*, or the second book, or at least the latter's most shocking passages, such as the apology for euthanasia, should be read as examples of *declamatio*, a rhetorical genre based on fictive, imagined arguments.[38] As a support for this hypothesis one might recall that More's *Utopia* was published twice, along with Erasmus's *Praise of Folly*, in Caspar Dornavius's seventeenth-century *Amphitheatrum sapientiae socraticae jocoseriae; hoc est, encomia et commentaria autorum, qua veterum, qua recentiorum prope omnium, quibus res, aut pro vilibus vulgo aut damnosis habitae, styli patrocinio vindicantur, exornantur, opus ad mysteria naturae discenda, ad omnem amoenitatem, sapientiam, virtutem, publice privatimque utilissimam*, an anthology made up largely of pieces written in jest by various writers (including Lucian) who praised fever, flies, nothingness, yes and no, and so forth.[39] Once again, the literal framework or context of More's *Utopia* was provided by Lucian and the Lucianic tradition. But in the case of Dornavius's *Amphitheatrum* there may have been an attempt to soften the aggressiveness of More's book by concealing it in a thick mass of innocuous pieces. Such a devious strategy suggests that a thorough investigation of the European reception of More's *Utopia* would be particularly rewarding, especially if it looked into indirect, below-the-surface evidence. Here is one admittedly conjectural example: In late 1524 Leonhard Reynmann published an astrological *Practica*, one of the many forecasts triggered by the imminent and ominous conjunction of all the planets under the sign of Pisces. The illustrated frontispiece showed Saturn, the pagan god, followed by a group of peasants flourishing their agricultural instruments as weapons; standing to one side, the pope and the emperor look frightened (fig. 1.4).

In a famous essay Aby Warburg commented on the presence of Saturn in the following terms: "The ancient god of seedtime was the natural emblem of his rebellious children."[40] But if the symbol was so obvious, why had it apparently never been used before? I wonder whether this aggressive depiction of the imminent return of the Golden Age as a symbol of social equality was not connected to the appearance, in that same year, 1524, of the German translation of the second book of

FIGURE 1.4. Leonhard Reynmann, frontispiece to *Practica* (1524). (Reprinted from C. Ginzburg, *Il nicodemismo: Simulazione e dissimulazione religiosa nell'Europa del '500* [Turin, 1970].)

More's *Utopia* (the first was tacitly ignored, as also happened with the Italian translation). Recall that Guillaume Budé's letter emphasized the suppression of greed that would have brought back the Golden Age of Saturn. Whether or not my hypothesis that Reynmann's frontispiece could have been a response to More's *Utopia* is correct, a larger question remains unanswered: how was More's *Utopia* read in Germany, on the eve of the Peasants War?

What we do know is how one rather special reader read *Utopia* in the New World about this time. Vasco de Quiroga, a judge, later bishop of Michoacán, used More's book as a blueprint for the reforms he introduced—including the communal ownership of goods—in two hospitals, or collective settlements, near Santa Fe. We still have the copy of More's *Utopia* used by Quiroga: its previous owner, Juan de Zumárraga, bishop of Mexico, had been a Franciscan friar deeply influenced by Erasmus.[41]

In a legal essay arguing that it was unlawful to keep Indians as slaves— *Información en derecho . . . sobre algunas provisiones del Real Consejo de Indias* (1535)— Quiroga says that More, "an illustrious gentleman, having a superhuman wit" (*varón ilustre y de ingenio más que humano*), had shown that the most naive populations of the New World were exactly like those of the Golden Age. "This writer, Thomas More, knew Greek very well," Quiroga explained. "He was an authoritative expert and translated from Greek into Latin some writings by Lucian, that describe laws, policies, and manners of the Golden Age and its naive populations, as one can see from what More says about these in his book on the commonwealth and Lucian about those in his *Saturnalia*."[42] A few pages earlier Quiroga had quoted a long passage from Lucian's *Saturnalia* in order to prove that both slavery and private property had been absent in that Golden Age that was so close to the "Golden Age of the New World."[43]

Vasco de Quiroga read More's *Utopia* and Lucian's *Saturnalia* as contiguous texts. Am I using Quiroga's interpretation as evidence to support my own interpretation of More? Yes and no. Such convergence does prove that my interpretation, though not necessarily correct, is certainly not anachronistic. But Quiroga's straightforward, one-dimensional reading of both More and Lucian is as distant as possible from their (especially More's) subtle, ironic shifting between fiction and reality. Did Quiroga misunderstand the complexity of More's and Lucian's texts, or was he simply using them as ammunition in his own legal battles? This issue does not concern me here. But the legal dimension is not inappropriate to a discussion on More's *Utopia*. The ancient legal term *monopolium* led More to see, by analogy, a new contemporary reality, *oligopolium*, although the English version of this word was not recognized by the *Oxford English Dictionary* until its most recent edition, presumably because it had been seen as a piece of economists' jargon.[44] On a general level, it is instructive to see that a myth, or *fabula* (as More himself called his *Utopia*), that had been inspired by Lucian's fictive arguments had a conceptual grip on reality, as legal *fictiones* often do.[45]

6

More's *Utopia* is a "bifocal book," R. J. Schoeck once wrote.[46] In a well-known essay, Stephen Greenblatt developed a brilliant comparison between More's *Utopia* and Holbein's *Ambassadors* (fig 1.5), claiming that the former's "subtle displacements, distortions, and shifts of perspective are the closest equivalent in Renaissance prose to the anamorphic virtuosity" of the latter. "The persona More and Hythlodaeus sit in the same garden and converse with each other, but as in Holbein's painting, they cast shadows in different directions and are, in crucial respects, necessarily blind to each other" Greenblatt remarks, hence the "sense . . . of incompatible perspectives between which the reader restlessly moves." This restlessness is certainly resonant to a late-twentieth-century reader, but can it explain *Utopia*'s powerful impact? This is what Greenblatt seems to suggest in his final remarks: "If, for over four hundred years, criticism has, more often than not, consisted of attempted seizures of the *libellus*—for the Church, the British Empire, the Revolution, or even Liberal Democracy—it is both because *Utopia* insists that any interpretation depends upon the reader's position and because the stakes seem surprisingly high."[47] Greenblatt is right in stressing that most interpreters have missed the "sense . . . of incompatible perspectives" that is so important in More's book. But, important as this formal element is, can we equate it with the core of the book?

The approach I have been advocating should take us beyond this dichotomy, since it encompasses both the "incompatible perspectives" stressed by Greenblatt and the much-debated "general frame" of the book. Among the peripheral effects of accepting this argument is a rejection of J. H. Hexter's theory of the "odd paragraph." According to Hexter (who is followed by most interpreters), the paragraph in the first book of *Utopia* promising a description of the island is a "seam" pointing to an earlier, ill-concealed stage of More's project, since no description is offered until the second book.[48] But in the framework of the Lucianic tradition that is so fond of textual and logical contradictions, Hexter's argument seems rather weak. "What happened in the other world I shall tell you in the succeeding books" reads the last sentence of the second, and last, book of Lucian's *True History*. "The biggest lie of all," a Greek scribe drily commented in the margin.[49]

I am aware that the contemporary scholar G. M. Logan dismissed the influence of Lucian, the satirist, as incompatible with "the all-too-sober passages in the account of Utopia." More's book, Logan warned us, "despite the wit and indirection of its manner, is a serious work of political philosophy."[50] But are the serious and comic elements in More's *Utopia* really opposed? In rejecting this kind of either/or interpretation, C. R. Thompson asked: "Why can't we have it both ways?"[51] Well, why not? The problem is how. What is at stake here is the relationship between the two sides of More's *Utopia*. Logan said "*despite* the wit and indirection of its manner"; I would say "*because*." More, as is well known, began by

FIGURE 1.5. Holbein, *The Ambassadors*, The National Gallery, London.

writing what would ultimately be the second book, the description of Utopia; he then added the first book, the description of England. On the basis of what I have said thus far I am pretty confident that in this case post hoc and propter hoc converge. Lucian's paradoxes must have played a crucial role in convincing More to change his original project, by showing him a field of possibilities.[52] Bizarre experiments in the mood of unreality suggested to him a framework for approaching reality from an unexpected angle, for asking oblique questions. What happens if, as Lucian once imagined, various philosophies are put up for sale?[53] What happens if private property is abolished? Ancient rituals of inversion such as Saturnalia helped More to imagine a fictitious society in which gold and silver were used to make chamber pots and foreign ambassadors were mistakenly assumed to be slaves. The same rituals of inversion helped him to see, for the first time, a paradoxical, inverted reality: an island where sheep devoured human beings.

CHAPTER TWO

Selfhood as Otherness: Constructing English Identity in the Elizabethan Age

"WHAT THE CHARACTER OF POETRY IS," the young Gerard Manley Hopkins once wrote, "will be found best by looking at the structure of verse. The artificial part of poetry, perhaps we shall be right to say all artifice, reduces itself to the principle of parallelism. The structure of poetry is that of continuous parallelism, ranging from the technical so-called Parallelisms of Hebrew poetry and the antiphons of Church music up to the intricacy of Greek or Italian or English verse."[1]

In quoting these words at the very beginning of a highly technical essay on "Grammatical Parallelism and Its Russian facet," Roman Jakobson emphasized the challenging comprehensiveness of Hopkins's approach.[2] I have chosen to start with the same passage in order to stress what this chapter will *not* be about. In the late sixteenth and early seventeenth centuries the relative "intricacy of Greek or Italian or English verse" became in many European countries, and especially in England, a debated issue. This story has been told before, but its implications deserve a further look.[3]

1

Consider a well-known example of a minor literary genre: Latin without tears. This is what Roger Ascham, tutor to Queen Elizabeth and Latin secretary to Queen Mary, promised in the lengthy title of a book published in 1570, two years after his death, *The scholemaster; or, Plaine and per-*

fite way of teachyng children, to understand, write, and speake, the latin tong, but specially purposed for the private brynging up of youth in Gentlemen and Noble mens houses, and commodious also for all such, as have forgot the Latin tonge, and would, by themselves, without a Scholemaster, in short tyme, and with small paines, recover a sufficient habilitie, to understand, write, and speake Latin.[4]

I do not know whether any youth ever succeeded either in learning or in recovering some Latin from Ascham's *Scholemaster.* But such a practical purpose was framed by a larger issue, which was not mentioned in the book's title. Sir Richard Sackville had asked Ascham "very earnestlie, to shewe, what [he] thought of the common goinge of Englishe men into Italie." This was a topic on which Ascham, a committed Protestant and a man of solid moral convictions, had strong opinions, having spent a few days in Venice some years earlier, an experience that left him with durable memories of sin. He highly praised "the Italian tonge, which next the Greeke and Latin tonge" he declared to "like and love above all other." But he contrasted the present state of Italy, and especially of Rome, with its respective past: "Tyme was, whan Italie and Rome, have bene, to the great good of us that now live, the best breeders and bringers up, of the worthiest men, not onelie for wise speakinge, but also for well doing, in all civill affaires, that ever was in the worlde. But now, that tyme is gone, and though the place remayne, yet the olde and present maners, do differ as farre, as blacke and white, as vertue and vice. . . . Italie now, is not that Italie, that it was wont to be" (23 r–v).

Ascham's argument for rejecting contemporary Italy was twofold. On the one hand, he stressed the moral corruption and religious incredulity of *Inglesi italianati,* those English gentlemen who, having spent some time in Italy, had absorbed its attitudes and behavior. On the other, he complained about the recent tide of English translations of Italian books. According to Ascham, they were "sold in every shop in London, commended by honest titles the soner to corrupt honest maners: dedicated over boldlie to vertuous and honorable personages, the easielier to begile simple and innocent wittes" (26 r–v). Ascham did not hesitate to urge "those, who have authoritie" to act to prevent the publication of further Italian translations, pointing to the fact that more of them had been "set out in Printe within these fewe monethes, than have bene sene in England many score yeare before."[5]

Ascham died in 1568. Two such works published in 1566 and 1567 more or less fit his description. One is William Painter's *The Palace of Pleasure*, dedicated to Ambrose, earl of Warwicke, and Sir George Howard, a two-volume selection taken from Boccaccio, Bandello, Livy, and other modern and classical authors that acquainted Elizabethan readers with such "pleasaunt Histories and Novelles" as those of *Coriolanus*, *Timon of Athens*, *The Duchess of Amalfi*, *Romeo and Juliet*, and *The Two Gentlemen of Venice*. Another is *The Historie of Ariodanto and Jenevra*, from Ariosto's *Orlando Furioso*. This last brings me to my current topic, the debate on rhyme.

2

"Rude beggerly ryming" Ascham wrote, had been "brought first into Italie by Gothes and Hunnes, where all good verses and all good learning to, were destroyd by them: and after caryed into France and Germanie: and at last receyved into England by men of excellent wit in deede, but of small learning, and less iudgement in that behalfe" (60 r).

This "attack on rhyme" was regarded by C. S. Lewis as "important only in so far as it was mischievous."[6] But a closer view suggests a less dismissive judgment. True, Ascham regarded rhyming as a barbarous, not to say beastly, feature: "To follow rather the Gothes in ryming than the Greekes in trew versifiying," he wrote, "were even to eate ackornes with swyne, when we may freely eate wheate bread emonges men" (60 r).

Today, this emotionally charged comparison may sound surprising. But, as Ernst Gombrich once aptly recalled, "The derivation of the word classical itself throws an amusing light on the social history of taste. For an *auctor classicus* is really a taxpaying author. Only people of standing belonged to one of the taxpaying classes in Roman society, and it was such people rather than 'proletarians' who spoke and wrote a type of educated language which the aspiring author was advised by the Roman Grammarian Aulus Gellius to emulate. In that sense the classic is really the 'classy.' "[7]

In the same spirit Ascham opposed the work of "the worthie Poetes in Athens and Rome, [who] were more carefull to satisfie the iudgement of one learned, than rashe in pleasing the humor of a rude multitude" to the baseness of what was to be found in "the shoppes in London . . . full of lewd and rude rymes"(60 v). His rejection of "beggerly, barbarous ryming" was part of a conscious effort to make England a truly civilized country, able to take the place of Italy as the worthiest heir to the Greek and Roman legacy, without falling into Italy's moral and religious corruption. In a revealing passage Ascham abandoned for once his customary reverence toward the Latin tradition and taxed Cicero for a comment on Britain he once made in a letter to Atticus. "There is not one scruple of silver in that whole isle," Cicero had written, "or any that knoweth either learnyng or letter" (*Ad Atticum*, IV, 17). Ascham bluntly replied: "But now master Cicero, blessed the God, and his sonne Jesu Christ, whom you never knew . . . it may trewly be sayd, that for silver, there is more cumlie plate, in one Citie of England, than is in foure of the proudest Cities in all Italie, and take Rome for one of them." Something similar, he went on, could be said about learning:

> And for learnyng, beside the knowledge of all learned tongs and liberall sciences, even your owne bookes Cicero, be as well read, and your excellent eloquence is as well liked and loved, and as trewlie folowed in England at this day, as it is now, or ever was, sence your owne tyme in any place of Italie. . . . And a litle to brag with you, Cicero, where you your selfe, by your leave, halted in

some point of learnyng in your owne tong, many in England at this
day go streight up, both in trewe skill, and right doing therein.

(62 r–v).

The idea that England could have exceeded Italy in the display of lux-
ury as well as in the love of Greek and Latin—in 1568—betrayed a remarkable amount of wishful thinking on Ascham's part, while the further allusion to English scholars having gone beyond Cicero's learning
was presumably a deliberate exaggeration. But Ascham's ambivalent attitude toward Italy can be detected in his warm praise of the metrical
experiments displayed by Felice Figliucci of Siena in his *De la filosofia
morale libri dieci, sopra li dieci libri de l'Ethica d'Aristotile:*

> Writyng upon Aristotles Ethickes so excellentlie in Italian, as never
> did yet any one in myne opinion either in Greke or Latin, amon-
> gest other thynges doth most earnestlie invey agaynst the rude
> ryming of verses in that tong: and whan soever he expresseth Aris-
> totles preceptes, with any example, out of Homer or Euripides, he
> translateth them, not after the Rymes of Petrarke, but into soch
> kinde of perfite verse, with like feete and quantitie of sillables, as
> he found them before in the Greke tonge: exhortyng earnestlie all
> the Italian nation, to leave of their rude barbariousnesse in ryming,
> and folow diligently the excellent Greke and Latin examples, in
> trew versifying.

According to Ascham, those Englishmen who "never went farder
than the schole of Petrarcke and Ariostus abroad, or els of Chaucer at
home" (61 v) should have taken Figliucci as a model instead.[8]

3

Ascham's passionate argument against rhyme, in favor of quantitative
verse, raised a considerable debate and a few dissenting voices. Among

the latter was Sir Philip Sidney, who in his *Apology for Poetry* (written ca. 1583) noticed, in a rather dismissive tone, that "there beeing in eyther [that is, either rhyme or quantitative verse] sweetness, and wanting in neither maiestie. Truly the English, before any other vulgar language, is fit for both sorts." But in stressing the reverence due to poetry "in all nations to this day," including Turkey and Ireland, Sidney remarked that "even among the most barbarous and simple Indians where no writing is, yet have their poets, who make and sing songs, which they call *Areytos*, both of theyr auncestors deedes and praises of their gods: a sufficient probabilitie that if ever learning come among them, it must be by having theyr hard dull wits softned and sharpened with the sweete delights of poetrie."[9]

This passage points at a significant, though little recognized side of the English debate on rhyme. I will try to clarify the implications of Sidney's remark by focusing on the word *aréytos*.

As has been noticed, the earliest account of *aréytos* in any European language occurs in Oviedo's *Historia general de las Indias* (first part, 1535). Notwithstanding their lack of writing, the Indians—Oviedo noticed—"kept memory of things past" through songs called *aréytos* based on their chiefs' or *caciques'* lives, which were accompanied by dances. Oviedo called *aréytos* "a sort of history," comparing them to the dances performed by the Etruscans on their visit to Rome, as described by Livy (VII, 2) and to Spanish and Italian vernacular songs based on historical events.[10] These parallels remind us of the obvious, that is, that sixteenth-century Europeans approached the New World through a conceptual framework rooted in their own societies, as well as in Greek and Roman antiquity. But the long-term effects of this encounter on both the European present and the European perception of the past is a rewarding topic of reflection.[11] The word I am talking about—*aréytos*—ultimately suggested the redefinition of a time-honored mode of conceptualizing history. In the introduction to his translation of Plutarch (one of the books that changed Europe forever), Jacques Amyot emphasized the antiquity and nobility of history, informing his readers that barbarous and illiterate populations from the West Indies were able to recall events eight hundred years old thanks to songs they had learned by heart in childhood.[12] A few years later Sebastian Fox Morzillo, the Spanish polymath, described a Mexican manuscript—the so-called Codex Mendoza, a gift to Emperor Charles the Fifth—that was decorated with images Morzillo compared to hieroglyphics. Though to him this was not writing, he grudgingly admitted that such an unwritten record of the past could be labeled "history" (*quam appellare historiam, licet non scriptam, possumus*).[13]

Neither Amyot nor Fox Morzillo mentioned *aréytos*. Sidney may have come across the French translation of Oviedo's book, published in Paris in 1557: *L'histoire naturelle et generale des Indes, isles et terre ferme de la grand mer Oceane*.[14] But a more likely source is, I would argue, François Bauduin's *De institutione historiae universae et eius cum iurisprudentia coniunctione* (The institution of universal history and its conjunction with jurisprudence), a treatise based on a series of lectures delivered by Bauduin, a famous law professor from Arras, at the University of Heidelberg. Bauduin's *De institutione*, first published in 1561, was included in *Artis historicae penus*, a two-volume anthology of writings on the art of history, published in Basel in 1579.[15] In October 1580 Sidney sent to his brother Robert a letter dealing with the writing of history that had presumably been inspired by the recent publication of the Basel anthology. Sidney likened the historian to a poet and more generally to "a Discourser, which name we give to who soever speakes '*non simpliciter de facto, sed de qualitatibus et circumstantiis facti*' " (not merely about a fact but about its features and circumstances).[16] Bauduin had used the same words in order to make the opposite point: historians had to go beyond the mere description of a fact and its circumstances (*factum aliquod . . . cum suis circumstantiis*), although they had to avoid the exaggerations of the "new rhetoricians," as well as the freedom of invention allowed to poets and artists (an echo of a famous line by

Horace).[17] But although Sidney did not agree with Bauduin's approach to history, the latter's treatise must have caught his attention.

Bauduin, originally a Catholic, had converted to Calvinism and become Calvin's secretary; later he returned to Catholicism and tried to act as a mediator between the two religions. His *De institutione*, dedicated to Antoine, king of Navarre, was written on the eve of the colloquy between Catholics and Calvinists at Poissy in September 1561. Bauduin himself played an important role at Poissy, which made him the presumable target of a virulent pamphlet written by Calvin immediately after: *Response à un cauteleux et rusé moyenneur* (Response to a cautious and shrewd mediator).[18] In his *De institutione* Bauduin addressed issues with inflammatory religious implications, such as the superiority of primary over secondary witnesses, in a broad comparative perspective. A similar topic examined in his treatise was the reliability of orally transmitted stories in a time and place without history as a literary genre. Bauduin started from the most ancient stage of Roman history, where, as one learns from Cicero's *Brutus*, banquet songs or *carmina*, already lost in Cicero's time, were sung to praise the deeds of famous men. Bauduin compared this passage with Tacitus, *Germania*, 2, 3 (*"Celebrant carminibus antiquis, quod unum apud illos memoriae et annalium genus est . . ."* [their ancient hymns—the only style of record or history that they possess]) and *Annales*, 2, 88, 3 (*"Caniturque adhuc barbaras apud gentes, Graecorum annalibus ignotus, quis sua tantum mirantur"* [and to this day (Arminius) is sung in tribal lays, though he is an unknown being to the Greek historians, who admire only the history of Greece). But what happened with ancient Germans, Bauduin went on, must have happened with other populations as well. He mentioned the passage in which Eginhardus describes Charlemagne transcribing and memorizing *barbara et antiquissima carmina* (barbarous and very ancient songs telling of the deeds of former kings and martial exploits). Then he added "I will recite another, and not less noble example" (*Recitabo alterum non minus nobile exemplum*) and told of the way newly discovered Indian populations transmitted the past, a method based either on series of drawings something like Egyptian hieroglyphics or on songs (*cantiones*) sung to accompany dances. These mixed songs with dancing (*choros*) are called *aréytos*, the word picked up by Sidney.[19]

I came across the passage from Bauduin in a footnote to Arnaldo Momigliano's splendid paper "Perizonius, Niebuhr and the Character of Early Roman Tradition," which analyzes how the discovery of a past transmitted orally by American Indians changed the perception of Roman history, giving rise to the so-called ballad theory.[20] But even Momigliano failed to appreciate fully Bauduin's remarks. What is so striking about them is both the broad comparative approach and the emphatically non-Eurocentric attitude. Having declared that American Indian songs provide a "not less noble" example than ancient Roman *carmina*, Bauduin commented, "*Nam et fas est et ab hoste doceri*" (Ovid, *Met.* 4, 428): "Learning is always legitimate, even from our enemies." But this translation of Ovid's line is misleading, since it inevitably misses the contiguity of *hostis*, "enemy," and *hospes*, "guest." Bauduin, a profound scholar of Roman law, was well aware that the old meaning of *hostis* was "alien," as in, for instance, the *Twelve Tables* passage *Adversus hostem aeterna auctoritas esto* (a property claim against an alien will never be abolished).[21] Having established that songs were used the world over to convey memories through time, Bauduin suggested a moral and political lesson: "Shall we be so degenerate as to refuse to hear the poem of our national history? And yet, in order to understand it we have to preserve the recollections of those who are usually labeled barbarians. Are we French, British, German, Spanish, or Italian? If we want to speak about ourselves we must not ignore the history of Franks, of Angles, of Saxons, of Goths, of Lombards. And since we have often fought Saracens and Turks, we must know Saracenic and Turkish history as well."[22]

These striking words seem to anticipate the scholarly program of eighteenth-century antiquarians like Muratori, not to mention the (often much more parochial) political and intellectual agenda of European nationalism.[23] In fact, for a long time French historians of law had been focusing on what we call the Middle Ages. But Bauduin reshaped this approach in a broad cosmopolitan perspective that embraced both barbarians and enemies, insofar as both were *hostes*, "alien." The defense of rhyme that emerged in England in the late-sixteenth and early-seventeenth centuries shared some of these assumptions.

4

In his reflections on the oral transmission of the past Bauduin implicitly undermined common assumptions about the hierarchical role of the classical tradition. The anonymous treatise *The Arte of English Poesie* (London, 1589), ascribed to George Puttenham, narrowed Bauduin's argument, transforming it into an attack on Greek and Latin verse. Puttenham's vivid words deserve to be quoted in full:

> It appeareth that our vulgar running Poesie was common to all the nations of the world besides, whom the Latines and Greekes in speciall called barbarous. So as it was, notwithstanding, the first and most ancient Poesie, and the most universall, which two points do otherwise give to all humane inventions and affaires no small credit. This is proved by certificate of marchants and travellers, who by late navigations have surveyed the whole world, and discovered large countries and strange people wild and savage, affirming that the American, the Perusine and the very Canniball, do sing and also say their highest and holiest matters in certaine riming versicles and not in prose, which proves also that our maner of vulgar Poesie is more ancient than the artificiall of the Greeks and Latines, ours comming by instinct of nature, which was before Art or observation, and used with the savage and uncivill, who were before all science or civilitie, even as the naked by prioritie of time is be-

fore the clothed, and the ignorant before the learned. The naturall Poesie therefore, being aided and amended by Art, and not utterly altered or obscured, but some signe left of it (as the Greekes and Latines have left none) is no lesse to be allowed and commended then theirs.[24]

Bauduin and Sidney had spoken of, respectively, *cantiones* and songs, not of rhyme. Neither of them had mentioned what became the cornerstone of Puttenham's argument, the opposition between nature and art. In fact, *The Arte of English Poesie* posited two sets of values: the first included that which is ancient, natural, barbarous (or savage), universal, naked, ignorant; the second, that which is recent, artificial, civil, particular, clothed, learned. The evidence about Puttenham's life is scarce, but he appears to have spent some time at the court of France.[25] Was Puttenham familiar with Montaigne's *Essays*, first published in 1580? An affirmative answer to this question is more than likely, since both *The Arte of English Poesie* and Montaigne's essay "On Cannibals" assign the word "barbarous," a crucial term in both texts, three different connotations: relative, negative, and positive.[26]

In the first place, "barbarous" is, according to Puttenham, a purely relative concept, being a derogatory word born of ethnic pride: "This terme grew by the great pride of the Greekes and Latines, when they were dominatours of the world, reckoning no language so sweete and civill as their owne, and that all nations beside them selves were rude and uncivill, which they called barbarous. . . . The Italian at this day by like arrogance calleth the Frenchman, Spaniard, Dutch, English, and all other breed behither their montaines *Appennines*, *Tramontani*, as who would say barbarous."[27]

This attitude did not prevent Puttenham from also using "barbarous" as a synonym for rude, rough, clumsy. In a digression on the history of rhyme—the earliest of its kind, as has already been noticed[28]—

Puttenham followed Ascham's suggestion, ascribing the corruption of "the Poesie metricall of the Grecians and Latines" to "the barbarous conquerers invading them with innumerable swarmes of strange nations" (ch. vi). But, presumably inspired by Bauduin's interest in those "barbarous and very ancient songs" mentioned by Eginhardus in his life of Charlemagne, Puttenham devoted a chapter of his work to a discussion of rhymed poetry written "in the times of Charlemaine and many yeares after him" (ch. vii). Predictably, Puttenham spoke of "excessive authoritie of Popes," "barbarous rudenes of the times," "idle invention of Monasticall men," and of a "fabulous age." A "large poem to the honour of Carolus Calvus, every word beginning with C," written by Hugobald the Monk, was—Puttenham commented—"no small peece of cunning . . . , though in truth it were but a phantasticall devise, and to no purpose at all more then to make them harmonicall to the rude eares of those barbarous ages." But in the chapter's final paragraph Puttenham provided a reason for dwelling on such clumsy literary products: "Thus you may see the humors and appetites of men, how divers and chaungeable they be in liking new fashions, though many tymes worse than the old, and not onely in the manner of their life and use of their garments, but also in their learninges and arts and specially of their languages."[29]

For a long time, garments, learning, arts, and languages had been regarded as topics relevant to antiquarians, not to historians. Even the link between rhyme and "humors and appetites," suggested by Puttenham, was not a novelty: in his *Scholemaster*, for instance, Roger Ascham had opposed the "lewd and rude rymes" that filled up London shops to the works of "the worthie Poetes in Athens and Rome, [who] were more carefull to satisfie the iudgement of one learned, than rashe in pleasing the humor of a rude multitude" (60 v). But Puttenham subverted the traditional hierarchy through his antiquarian curiosity, transforming rhymes, which used to be dismissed as barbarous, into a legitimate research topic.[30] Fifty years later Jean Chapelain, the French poet and critic, argued for the historical relevance of a medieval romance like *Lancelot* in terms that revealed some of the implications of Puttenham's remark: "Physicians analyze their patients' corrupted humours on the basis of their dreams: in the same way, we can analyze the customs and manners of the past on the basis of the phantasies described in their writings."[31] Both social history and *histoire des mentalités* would ultimately emerge from this sort of antiquarian research.

But "barbarous" had for Puttenham, and for Montaigne as well, a third, positive significance. Rhyme, being "uncivill" (that is, barbarous) and universal, is "naturall."[32] But even "naturall Poesie," according to Puttenham, had to be "aided and amended by Art, and not utterly altered or obscured, but some signe left of it (as the Greekes and Latines have left none)" (ch v). In the last section of *The Arte of English Poesie* Puttenham clarified this compromise by rephrasing his opposition between nature and art, starting from his opening argument: that the poet is, etymologically, a maker. Being a maker, Puttenham concluded, he is comparable to a carpenter, a painter, a carver, or a gardener. But only to a certain extent:

> But for that in our maker or Poet, which restes onely in devise and issues from an excellent sharpe and quick invention, holpen [helped] by a cleare and bright phantasie and imagination, he is not as the painter to counterfaite the naturall by the like effects and not the same, nor as the gardiner aiding nature to worke both the same and the like, nor as the carpenter to worke effectes utterly unlike, but even as nature her selfe working by her owne peculiar vertue and proper instinct and not by example and meditation or exercise as all other artificers do, is then most admired when he is most naturall and least artificiall.[33]

The artist as a creator: in emphasizing the Neoplatonic roots of this notion M. H. Abrams quoted a few parallel passages by Sidney and

Puttenham.[34] One might also recall that in 1585 Giordano Bruno had published in London his *De gli heroici furori*, with a dedication to Philip Sidney.[35] The Neoplatonic elements in Puttenham's *Arte of English Poesie* are clear enough, but I wonder whether in praising poetry "as nature her selfe" Puttenham was not also echoing Castiglione's *sprezzatura*, that is, spontaneity recovered through art and beyond art. This would explain why Puttenham, after a chapter entitled "What it is that generally makes our speach well pleasing & commendable, and of that which the Latines call Decorum," went on to discuss courtly behavior in a chapter entitled "Of decencie in behaviour, which also belongs to the consideration of the Poet or maker."[36]

5

"This brutish Poetrie . . . I meane this tynkerly verse which we call ryme," wrote William Webbe in his *Discourse of English Poetrie*, published in 1586.[37] These words ought to be kept in mind in order to catch the polemical edge to Puttenham's concern for social and stylistic decorum, his eagerness to make rhyme—his stress on its natural, barbarous, wild features notwithstanding—a respectable, even courtly device. Samuel Daniel, in his *Defence of Ryme* (1603), developed these apparent contradictions in a new direction.[38]

The year before, Thomas Campion had published his *Observations in the Art of English Poesie*, arguing that classical meters fitted the English tongue better than the "vulgar and unarteficiall custome of ryming."[39] Daniel addressed Campion's technical arguments only in the final section of his *Defence of Ryme*; the bulk of his answer focused on larger issues. Daniel started by bluntly reversing the superiority of art over nature posited by Campion. "Custome that is before all Law, Nature that is above all Arte," he wrote. Then he unfolded the implications of these uncompromising words: "All our understandings are not to be built by the square of *Greece* and *Italie*. We are the children of nature as well as they. . . . All their Poesie, all their Philosophie is nothing, unlesse we bring the discerning light of conceipt with us to apply it to use. It is not bookes, but onely that great booke of the world, and the all overspreading grace of heaven that makes men truely iudiciall."[40]

The next paragraph of Daniel's text included a nearly literal quotation from Montaigne's essay "On Cannibals."[41] Although Montaigne's name was not mentioned, no contemporary reader was likely to have missed the echo of his powerful voice in the passage. The first English translation of Montaigne's *Essais* was published in 1603, the same year Daniel's pamphlet appeared. Daniel had been involved in this project, both directly and indirectly, through the translator, John Florio, who was his brother-in-law and close friend. Daniel dedicated to Florio a long poem on Montaigne, praising him, among other things, for having "made such bolde sallies out upon / *Custome*, the mightie tyrant of the earth, / In whose *Seraglio* of subiection / We all seeme bred-up, from our tender birth."[42]

Florio's Montaigne was Shakespeare's Montaigne. The utopian commonwealth described in act 2, scene 1, of *The Tempest* ("no kind of traffic / would I admit; no name of magistrates") was inspired by Florio's translation of the essay "On Cannibals."[43] Were Montaigne's essays on primitivism unusually appealing to English readers? In Italy, for instance, where Montaigne's *Essais* had been translated in 1590, the impact of those reflections was minimal.[44] This divergence, albeit far from unpredictable, might tell us something about the English reception of Montaigne.

In commenting on the Italian translation of Montaigne, Carlo Dionisotti called it "a decisive turning point," insofar as it showed that "a new era had begun in the history of the literary relationship between Italy and France. . . . Italy was at last becoming aware of the existence and predominance of a new system based on continental Europe."[45] The English translation of Montaigne, which also came from an Italian intellectual environment, adds a twist to this conclusion. John Florio, the translator, was, like his father, a Protestant exile from Italy. In his introductory address, Florio recalled that some people regarded translations as "the subversion of Universities"; he then quoted his "olde fellow Nolano" who had said and publicly taught that "from translation all Science had its of-spring," since the Greeks had drawn all their science from the·Egyptians, who had taken it from the "Hebrews or Chaldees." "Nolano" was of course Giordano Bruno of Nola, who had been burned in Rome as a heretic three years earlier. John Florio, one of the characters of Bruno's dialogue *La cena de le Ceneri*, evoked his dead friend with words that fit the image of the Hermetic magus Frances Yates captured for us.[46] But intellectual subordination to France, demonstrated in Dionisotti's view by the Italian translation of Montaigne, is clearly absent in the English translation. I would say even the opposite. Montaigne, who may seem today the epitome of literary Frenchness, played a relevant role in the self-assertion of an English identity *against* "a new system based on continental Europe," centered on France.

This English reading of Montaigne is present in Puttenham's *The Arte of English Poesie* and, even more explicitly, in Daniel's *Defence of Ryme*. The rejection of the traditional emphasis on the Greek and Roman legacy, the stress on barbarous artifacts like rhyme, led Daniel to question—in a genuine Montaignesque spirit—European superiority as a whole: "Will not experience confute us, if wee shoulde say the state of *China*, which never heard of Anapestiques, Trochies, and Tribracques, were grosse, barbarous, und uncivile?" (Hr). But Daniel struck a note that is definitely absent from Montaigne, the vindication of what we call the Middle Ages: "The *Gothes*, *Vandales* and *Longobards*, whose comming downe like an inundation overwhelmed, as they say, al the glory of learning in *Europe*, have yet left us still their lawes and customes, as the originalls of most of the provinciall constitutions of Christendome" (Hr).

Daniel raised doubts concerning a contemporary notion that Latin had been revived by Reuchlin, Erasmus, and More. Long before them Petrarch had written excellent Latin verse and prose, even though it was his vernacular poetry that earned him glory and renown in his own country. Daniel mentioned an impressive list of Italian humanists who had followed in Petrarch's footsteps. Then he added: "And yet long before all these, and likewise with these, was not our Nation behind in her portion of spirite and worthinesse, but cuncurrent with the best of all this lettered worlde" (Hr).

Daniel quotes Bede, Walter Map, Bracton, Bacon, Ockham, "and an infinite Catalogue of excellent men, most of them living about foure hundred yeares since, and have left behinde them monuments of most profound iudgement and learning in all sciences. So that it is but the clowds gathered about our owne iudgement that makes us thinke all other ages wrapt up in mists, and the great distance betwixt us, that causes us to imagine men so farre off, to be so little in respect of our selves" (H2r).

Daniel's antiquarian piety included obscure names, such as Aldelmus Durotelmus, praised as " the best poet of his times," who flourished in the year 739. Occasionally Daniel's vindication of the Middle Ages took him outside England: "Erasmus, Rewcline and More brought no more wisdome into the world with all their new revived wordes then we finde was before, it bred nor a profunder Divine than Saint *Thomas*, a greater Lawyer than *Bartolus*, a more accute Logician than *Scotus*" (H2v). But then he switched again to his major concern: "Let us go no further, but looke upon the wonderfull Architecture of this state of *England*, and see whether they were deformed times, that could give it such a forme" (H2v).

There is no need to go on, since Daniel's text is well known—by far the best known in the whole debate on rhyme. Daniel's vindication of those "deformed times"—the Middle Ages—has impressed all interpreters because of its sheer originality.[47] But Daniel's attitude becomes less surprising if reinserted in the context I have suggested. "Shall we be so degenerate as to refuse to hear the poem of our national history?"

François Bauduin had written in his *De institutione historiae universae*. "And yet, in order to understand it," he went on, "we have to preserve the recollection of those who are usually labelled barbarians. Are we French, British, German, Spanish, or Italian? If we want to speak about ourselves we must not ignore the history of Franks, of Angles, of Saxons, of Goths, of Lombards." In his *Defence of Ryme* Daniel revived, from an entirely English angle, the course sketched by Bauduin.

6

At the beginning of this century Daniel's *Defence of Ryme* was regarded as an anticipation of romanticism.[48] We can easily guess the source of such an anachronistic evaluation: Daniel was anticlassic, therefore he could be regarded as modern. "Modern" is of course a slippery word, but in this case one can be more specific. The *querelle des anciens et des modernes* did not start in France; it started in England, triggered by the debate on rhyme. One of the themes in this debate was precisely the relationship between England and the Continent: between England and France, as well as, on a more symbolic level, between England and Italy. The rejection of quantitative verse based on Greek and Latin models in favor of rhyme led to a declaration of intellectual independence from the continent. "Barbarous" became a positive word, a sign of pride.

And then, Fernand Braudel once wrote, England became an island.[49] Ironically, the historian who associated his name with *longue durée* was referring to a typical *événement*, albeit one with a symbolic value: the French conquest of Calais. What one might call the insularization of England was, however, a process not an event: a long process, involving self-reflection that took place on many levels. As I have tried to show, the defense of rhyme played a minor but distinctive role in it.

CHAPTER THREE

A Search for Origins:
Rereading Tristram Shandy

1

THE TOPIC HERE, Laurence Sterne's *Tristram Shandy*, seems at first glance unrelated to the previous ones, but only apparently so. First, all my "glimpses of English literature in a world perspective," as the subtitle of this volume reads, share a reference to an island—either fictitious, as with More's *Utopia*, or real, like England—seen through different textual frames from a noninsular perspective. Second, and more important, each chapter focuses on the relationship between fictional and nonfictional narratives, stressing—against the commonplace that all narratives are ultimately fictional—their intricate, often contentious exchanges. More's imaginary island, I have argued, led him to look at English society and its recent developments from a deeply unconventional perspective. In the second chapter, I showed how at an early stage of the English conquest of the world, some writers defended rhyme as a barbarous device, stressing the insularization of England compared to the European continent. In this chapter I will look at the relationship between fictional and nonfictional texts from a different angle, although again from a noninsular perspective.

The first six volumes of *The Life and Opinions of Tristram Shandy* appeared in quick succession during 1760 and 1761 and met with enormous success. At the end of the sixth volume, chapter 40, Sterne cast a retrospective glance at his book in progress. This passage is familiar to every reader of Sterne's book, and it provides us with an appropriate starting point:

> I am now beginning to get fairly into my work; and by the help of a vegetable diet, with a few of the cold seeds, I make no doubt but I shall be able to go on with my uncle Toby's story, and my own, in a tolerable straight line. Now,

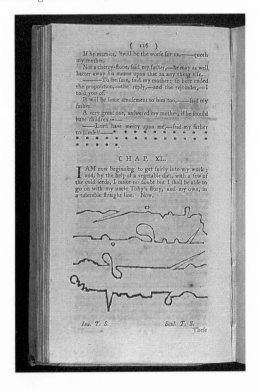

FIGURE 3.1. L. Sterne, *The Life and Opinions of Tristram Shandy*, in *The Works* (London, 1779), 2:116.

These were the four lines I moved in through my first, second, third, and fourth volumes—In the fifth volume I have been very good,—the precise line I have described in it being this:

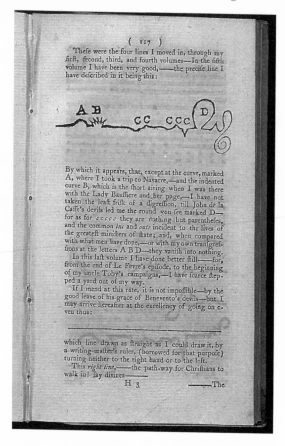

FIGURE 3.2. L. Sterne, *The Life and Opinions of Tristram Shandy*, in *The Works* (London, 1779), 2:117.

By which it appears, that except at the curve, marked A. where I took a trip to Navarre,—and the indented curve B. which is the short airing when I was there with the Lady Baussiere and her page,—I have not taken the least frisk of a digression, till John de la Casse's devils led me the round you see marked D.—for as for *c c c c c* they are nothing but parentheses, and the common *ins* and *outs* incident to the lives of the greatest ministers of state; and when compared with what men have done,—or with my own transgressions of the letters A B D—they vanish into nothing.

In this last volume I have done better still—for from the end of Le Fever's episode, to the beginning of my uncle Toby's campaigns,—I have scarce stepped a yard out of my way.

If I mend at this rate, it is not impossible—by the good leave of his grace of Benevento's devils—but I may arrive hereafter at the excellency of going on even thus; which is a line drawn as straight as I could draw it, by a writing-master's ruler, (borrowed for that purpose) turning neither to the right hand or to the left.

This *right line*,—the path-way for Christians to walk in! say divines—

—The emblem of moral rectitude! says Cicero—

—The *best line*! say cabbage planters—is the shortest line, says Archimedes, which can be drawn from one given point to another.—[1]

Before commenting on this passage, I want to clarify the ironical description of the sixth volume, where, the narrator says, "I have scarce stepped a yard out of my way." The volume includes, among other things, a digression generated by a discussion between Mr. and Mrs. Shandy about their child's breeches, which fills the entirety of chapter 19. It starts:

After my father had debated the affair of the breeches with my mother,—he consulted Albertus Rubenius upon it; and Albertus Rubenius used my father ten times worse in the consultation (if

possible) than even my father had used my mother: For as Rubenius had wrote a quarto *express, De re Vestiaria Veterum,*—it was Rubenius's business to have given my father some lights.—On the contrary, my father might as well have thought of extracting the seven
cardinal virtues out of a long beard,—as of extracting a single word
out of Rubenius upon the subject.

Upon every article of ancient dress, Rubenius was very commu-
nicative to my father;—gave him a full and satisfactory account of
The Toga, or loose gown.

The Chlamys.

The Ephod.

The Tunica, or Jacket. . . .[2]

The list goes on for two pages, shifting from breeches to shoes.

Undoubtedly, the reader who read these two passages in 1761 was
confronted with a very strange phenomenon, which deliberately trans-
gressed his or her implicit expectations of what a book could be. The
artifact still looks very strange indeed. Is *Tristram Shandy* a novel? And
what made *Tristram Shandy* possible?

2

In 1917 Viktor Shklovsky, one of the most prominent figures in Russian
formalism, answered this question in the most uncompromising way:
"*Tristram Shandy* is the most typical novel in world literature," he wrote in
the conclusion to the essay "The Novel as Parody: Sterne's *Tristram
Shandy,*" included in his collection *Theory of Prose.*[3] These words sound
much less shocking than they did eighty years ago; today many more
people would be ready to identify narrative self-reflexivity as the trade-
mark of the novelistic genre, and *Don Quixote* as the first modern novel.
Shklovsky, who was not particularly interested in the question "what
made *Tristram Shandy* possible?" mentioned the name of Cervantes. Here

he was simply following in the footsteps of Sterne himself, who, in his own unmistakable way, once had evoked his literary ancestors: "By the tombstone of Lucian—if it is in being,—if not, why then, by his ashes! by the ashes of my dear Rabelais, and dearer Cervantes. . . ."[4]

Some of the most prominent and disconcerting features in the two passages just presented can be regarded as offspring of, respectively, Rabelais (the mocking use of erudition) and Cervantes (the intrusive presence of the narrative voice).[5] And certainly both Rabelais and Cervantes would have been inconceivable without the rediscovery of Lucian of Samosata made by Erasmus and Thomas More at the very beginning of the sixteenth century. But neither Rabelais nor Cervantes (or, by the way, Lucian) can be invoked as having set precedents for the most blatant feature of *Tristram Shandy*: the absence of a real plot. The motto of the seventh volume (taken from Pliny the Younger, V, 6) can be applied to *Tristram Shandy* as a whole: *Non enim excursus hic eius, sed opus ipsum est* (This is not a digression from the main work but the work itself). Sterne shared Hogarth's conviction that beauty means variety and its line is serpentine; he might have endorsed the motto ascribed to William Kent, the creator of the English garden, that "nature abhors a strait line."[6] *Tristram Shandy* is a novel made of unpredictable digressions.[7] So what made it possible?

3

"Locke's *Essay Concerning Human Understanding*," Graham Petrie wrote, echoing what has been for a long time a widely shared assumption, "put forward theories of the sequence of ideas which profoundly influenced Sterne and which are the basis of much of the seemingly arbitrary structure of *Tristram Shandy*."[8] This judgment seems to be based on Sterne's comment that the association between winding a clock and sexual intercourse described at the beginning of the novel is the sort of "strange combination of ideas" that "the sagacious Locke, who certainly understood the nature of these things better than most men, affirms to have produced more wry actions than all other sources of prejudice whatsoever."[9] But is this remark sufficient to ascribe the peculiar structure of *Tristram Shandy* to the impact of Locke's thought, as many scholars have argued against a few dissenting voices?

Another piece of evidence, of a very different kind, seems to give a more explicit echo of Sterne's self-judgment of his relationship with Locke; it is drawn from the memoirs of Dominique-Joseph Garat, a minor French writer and politician, published in Paris in 1821. Garat reports a conversation that took place in Paris half a century before between Sterne and Jean-Baptiste-Antoine Suard, Hume's French translator. Sterne, requested to explain the secret of his originality, mentioned three things: (1) his own imagination and sensibility; (2) daily reading of the Bible; and (3) a "prolonged study of Locke, which he had begun in youth and continued through life. Anyone, he told Suard, who was acquainted with Locke, might discover the philosopher's directing hand 'in all his pages, in all his lines, in all his expressions.' "[10] Locke's philosophy is then defined as "a philosophy too religious to dare to explain the miracle of sensations . . . a holy philosophy, without which neither a true universal religion, nor a true morality, nor a genuine mastery of mankind over nature would ever be possible."[11]

It is unclear whether the comment about Locke's holy philosophy had been made by Sterne, by Suard, or by Garat.[12] In fact, the whole account sounds unreliable, being so indirect; moreover, too many things had occurred both in France and in Europe since the alleged conversation between Sterne and Suard in 1764. In the political atmosphere of the Restoration it was too tempting to present Locke as a pious, restrained philosopher, the very opposite of the bold *philosophes* who had allegedly set the stage for the Revolution. It would be better to leave aside this dubious and peripheral evidence. The voice of Yorick, Sterne's authorial alter ego, suggests a less deferential attitude: "Wit and judgment in this world never go together; inasmuch as they are two operations differing from each other as wide as east is from west.—So, says Locke,—so are farting and hickuping, say I."[13]

According to J. Traugott, the author of the book *Sterne's Philosophical Rhetoric*, Locke's *Essay on Human Understanding* was the "formal cause of *Tristram*." But even Traugott ultimately admits that the latter's "digressions (and there is nothing else in the book) must be brought on by some association of ideas—doubtless they are, since to connect ideas is to associate them—but it is not Locke's association of ideas." The same critic spoke of "Sterne's skeptical development of Locke."[14] If Locke's *Essay* is, as I believe, a false trail, in what direction should we turn to find, if not the "formal cause," at least the literary challenge that made Sterne's project possible?

4

My answer is this: *Tristram Shandy* is basically a fictionalized response to a set of options provided by Pierre Bayle's *Dictionnaire historique et critique*, both in its content and in its peculiar structure. The connections between Sterne and Bayle have been pointed out before. Some time ago, in a pathbreaking but largely ignored article, F. Doherty explored the influence on Sterne of the English translation of Bayle's *Dictionary*, which he had borrowed in 1752 from the Minster Library and kept on loan for ten months. "From what evidence I have been able to assemble," Doherty wrote, "Sterne saw and enjoyed the joke of using scurrilous or obscene snippets from the *Dictionary* to complicate his own telling of a tale in *Tristram Shandy*, looked on the vast work as another monument to man's absurdity, and saw the parade of learning as a worthy counterpart to Burton's *Anatomy of Melancholy*. But, more than this," he went on, "because Mr. Shandy is just the kind of man whom Tristram would associate with this kind of quaint scholarship and weighty substance, Sterne enjoys using Bayle against 'my father.'"[15]

I would leave aside the last observation, since the narrator's point of view may not coincide with Sterne's. Doherty's conclusions differ from mine, largely because they deal only with the novel's content, ignoring its formal structure. I argue that in that structure Sterne's use of Bayle had a purpose beyond merely "complicat[ing] his own telling of a tale in *Tristram Shandy*," as Doherty said. I focus on three issues: (a) digressions; (b) obscenities; and (c) the handling of time.

5

Bayle's fondness for digressions is well known. In his *Pensées diverses sur la comète* he proudly confessed: "I do not know what a regular reflection is; I am always ready to change; I often leave aside my subject; I jump into places following unpredictable by-ways, and a doctor who wants regularity and method everywhere would easily lose patience with me."[16] These habits found an appropriate outlet in the enterprise that made Bayle's name famous all over Europe, his *Dictionnaire historique et critique*. Bayle's original project seemed unambitious: a list of factual mistakes he had found in earlier encyclopedias, such as Moreri's. Years of incessant, lonely work produced four folio volumes, totaling 3,269 pages in the edition I consulted, published in Basel in 1741, most of which were in small print, for reasons I will explain shortly. Each of them was shaped by Bayle's passion for truth, starting from factual truth.[17] Figure 3.3 reproduces a page of Bayle's *Dictionary*.

The text of each entry is surrounded by a three-tiered system of footnotes: lowercase *a*, *b*, *c*, and so on for footnotes to the main text; uppercase *A*, *B*, *C*, etc., for longer remarks; and footnotes numbered 1, 2, 3, and up on the remarks. Sometimes, for the sake of clarity, additional typographical signs, such as asterisks or crosses, were added as well.

The clever typographical arrangement of Bayle's *Dictionary* was an improved version of two previous, authoritative, and possibly related models: the annotated Bible, inspired by the Talmud, and the annotated

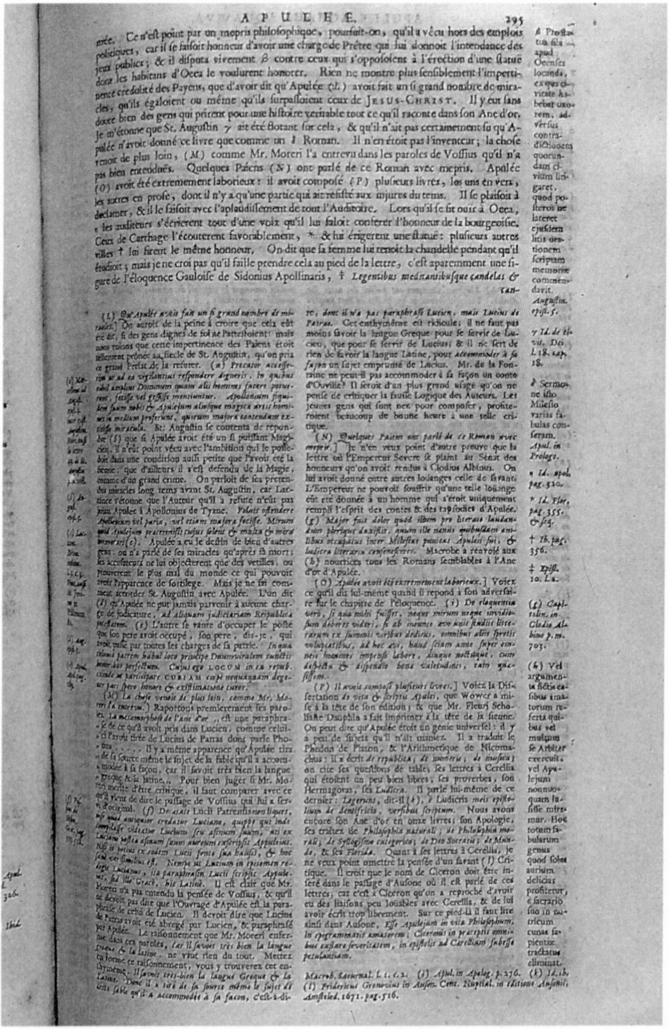

FIGURE 3.3. A page of Bayle's *Dictionary*.

Digestum, the great collection of Roman laws inspired by the emperor Justinian (figs. 3.4 and 3.5).[18] But these typographical analogies are ultimately deceptive. In the Bible, in the Talmud, and in the *Digestum*, the relationship between text and comments is centripetal, being focused on the text. In Bayle's *Dictionary* the relationship between text and footnotes is centrifugal. Des Maizeaux, in his deferential biography of Bayle, admitted that "sometimes the Text seems to have been made for the sake of the Remarks."[19] It was true that Bayle often concealed his boldest skeptical remarks in long footnotes appended to some peripheral articles. But he regarded the search for a truth, albeit peripheral and minuscule, as an aim in itself. For Bayle, truth was, so to speak, indivisible. The *Dictionary*'s typographical arrangement gives every reader the opportunity to check Bayle as he checks every date, every quotation, every piece of information, and to share Bayle's regressive and digressive path toward the sources of truth (or of error). But Bayle always remains the absolute master of the game: he acts like a despot, impervious to both limits and constraints. A given entry in his *Dictionary* can go on for more than eighteen folio pages (as does the one on Spinoza) or for a few lines. In the maze of the footnotes all sorts of topics can suddenly crop up: for instance, a discussion of Descartes's cosmology in the entry on "Ovid" or a debate on the possibility of leading a virtuous life without believing in God's providence in the entry on "Sommona-Codom," dedicated to an obscure religious man from Siam.

Sterne's novel shares Bayle's freedom and lack of constraints. And Tristram Shandy's search for his own origins as a human being follows a regressive and digressive pattern that transposes the erratic path of Bayle's erudite research to a fictional level.[20] Sterne's diagrams are in fact a jocular homage to Bayle's *Dictionary*. The double notation system (*A*, *c*) echoes Bayle's three-tiered system (fig. 3.2). Moreover Doherty dug out a hidden allusion to Bayle's *Dictionary* in Sterne's comment on the diagram: "I have not taken the least frisk of a digression, till John de la

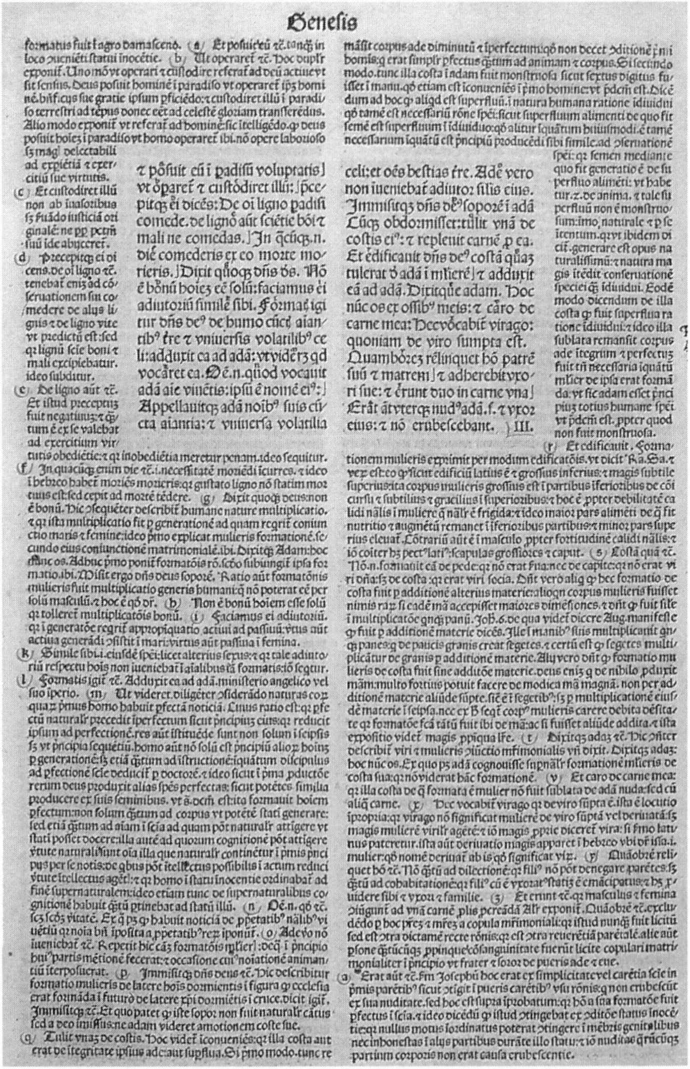
Genesis

ꝛ pôsuit eũ i padisũ voluptatis] vt ôparet ꝛ custôdiret illũ:]pcepitqꝫ ẽi dicẽs: De oĩ ligno padisi comede. de lignô aũt sciẽtie bõi ꝛ mali ne comedas.] In q̄cũqꝫ.n. diẽ comederis ex eo morte morieris.] Dixit quoqꝫ dñs ds. Nô ẽ bõnũ hoĩez eẽ solũ: faciamus ẽi adiutoriũ similẽ sibi. Formatꝭ igitur dñs deꝰ de humo cũctꝭ aiantibꝰ ŧre ꝛ vniuersis volatilibꝰ celi: adduxit ea ad adã: vt viderꝫ qd vocaret ea. Oẽ.n. qñod vocauit adã aĩe viuẽtis: ipsũ ẽ nomẽ eiꝰ:] Appellauitqꝫ adã noĩbꝰ suis cũcta aiantia: ꝛ vniuersa volatilia celi: et oẽs bestias ŧre. Adẽ vero non iueniebaŧ adiutor silis eius. Immisitqꝫ dñs deꝰ soporẽ i adã. Cũqꝫ obdormisset: tulit vnã de costis eiꝰ: ꝛ repleuit carnẽ ꝓ ea. Et ẽdificauit dñs deꝰ costã q̊̃az tulerat ð adã i mlierẽ] ꝛ adduxit eã ad adã. Dixitq̊ꝫ adam. Hoc nũc os ex ossibꝰ meis: ꝛ câro de carne mea: Hec vôcabiŧ virago: quoniam de viro sumpta est. Quambõrez rẽlinquet hõ patrẽ suũ ꝛ matrem] ꝛ adherebit vxori sue: ꝛ ẽrunt duo in carne vna] Erât ãt vterqꝫ nudꝰ adã. s. ꝛ vxor eius: ꝛ nõ erubescebant.] III.

FIGURE 3.4. A page of Nicholas de Lyra's *Postilla*.

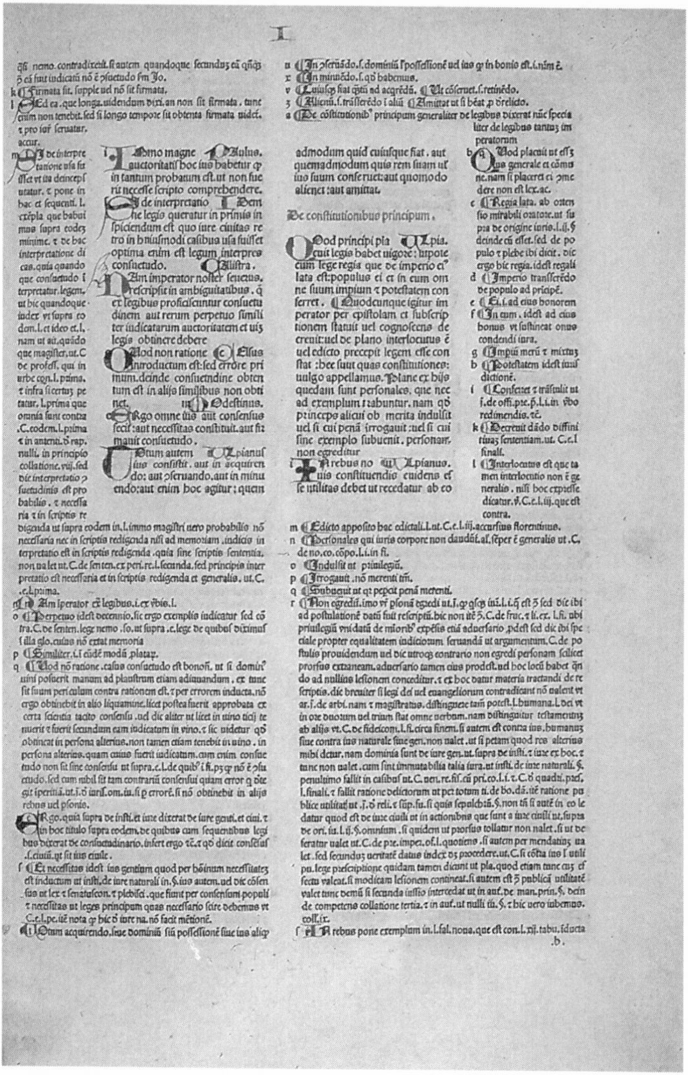
I

Nemo magne [Paulus.] auctoritatis hoc ius habetur q in tantum probatum est. ut non fuerit necesse scripto comprehendere. ¶ De interpretatio [Idem] Si de interpretatione legis queratur in primis inspiciendum est quo iure ciuitas retro in huiusmodi casibus usa fuisset optima enim est legum interpres consuetudo. [Calistra.] Nam imperator noster Seuerus. rescripsit in ambiguitatibus. que ex legibus proficiscuntur consuetudinem aut rerum perpetuo similiter iudicatarum auctoritatem uim legis obtinere debere ¶ Quod non ratione [Celsus] introductum est: sed errore primum. deinde consuetudine obtentum est in aliis similibus non obtinet. [Modestinus.] Ergo omne ius aut consensus fecit: aut necessitas constituit. aut firmauit consuetudo. [Ulpianus] Totum autem ius consistit. aut in acquirendo: aut conseruando. aut in minuendo: aut enim hoc agitur: quemadmodum quid cuiusque fiat. aut quemadmodum quis rem suam uel ius suum conseruet: aut quomodo alienet: aut amittat.

De constitutionibus principum.

Quod principi placuit [Ulpia.] legis habet uigorem: utpote cum lege regia que de imperio eius lata est: populus ei et in eum omne suum imperium et potestatem conferret. ¶ Quodcunque igitur imperator per epistolam et subscriptionem statuit uel cognoscens decreuit: uel de plano interlocutus est uel edicto precepit legem esse constat: hee sunt quas constitutiones uulgo appellamus. Plane ex his quedam sunt personales. que nec ad exemplum trahuntur. nam quod princeps alicui ob merita indulsit uel si cui penam irrogauit: uel si cui sine exemplo subuenit. personam non egreditur [Ulpianus.] In rebus nouis constituendis euidens esse utilitas debet ut recedatur ab eo

FIGURE 3.5. A page of the *Digestum Vetus* (Venice, 1488–90).

Casse's devils led me the round you see marked D." John de la Casse is Giovanni della Casa, archbishop of Benevento, the author of *Il Galateo*, the famous book on etiquette. As Bayle recalled in a scandalized tone (hardly masking his obvious relish), Archbishop della Casa had written a poem in his youth, *Capitolo del forno* (The oven), where he admitted to having occasionally indulged in sodomy.[21]

6

This leads me to my next topic: obscenities. Every reader of *Tristram Shandy* will be grateful to Doherty for having clarified Sterne's nearly private joke. But the point I would like to make about obscenities is a larger one, since it is related to the novel's construction not to the content of a specific passage.

Bayle spiced many entries of his *Dictionary* with long (and often extremely funny) quotations, usually in Latin, dealing with sexual matters. Rightly or wrongly, Elisabeth Labrousse detected behind them some traces of a puritanical attitude toward sex.[22] Bayle produced a long explanation (more than twenty folio pages in the English translation) bearing the title "That if there are some obscenities in this book, they are such as cannot be justly censured."[23] To those who argued that writers should refrain from using indecent words or lewd expressions, Bayle objected by pushing the argument to an extreme. He relied on Molière's play *La Critique de l'Ecole des Femmes*, where a group of *précieuses* engage in a debate on the alleged bawdiness of the author's previous play, *L'Ecole des Femmes*: "Those obscenities, God be thanked," one *précieuse* says, "appear bare-faced, they have not the least covering: the boldest eyes are frighted at their nakedness. . . . That passage of the scene, wherein Agnes mentions what was got from her, is more than sufficient to prove what I say. Fy . . . Is not modesty visibly offended by what Agnes says in the place we speak of?"

Another *précieuse* replies: "Not at all. Agnes does not say a word but what is very modest; and if you will have it, that she means something else, the obscenity proceeds from you, and not from her, for she speaks only of a ribbon that one got from her."

"Ah! you may talk of a ribbon as much as you please; but that *my* where she stops, was not put there for nothing: it occasions strange thoughts; that *my* is furiously scandalous; and say what you will you can never justify the insolence of that *my*. There is an intolerable obscenity in it."[24]

Bayle commented on this dialogue twice, in quick succession. In a footnote he wrote: "I am to observe that, in this passage of Molière, every body expects to hear Agnes say, that some body has got her maidenhead; which excites a very obscene idea." Therefore, Bayle went on in the main text, "that discourse, though never so impertinent, would be proper and honest, according to this principle, *All words which defile the imagination, that is to say, which denote an obscene object, ought to be laid aside.*"[25]

Having unfolded the absurd implications of this principle, Bayle triumphantly concluded that there was no difference between the most obscene and the most bashful language, since everything depends on the reader's (or listener's) reactions. Sterne explored this idea in many ways: from the white page where the reader of *Tristram Shandy* is asked to draw the alluring features of Widow Wadman ("Sit down, Sir, paint her to your own mind—as like your mistress as you can—as unlike your wife as your conscience will let you—'tis all one to me—please but your own fancy in it")[26] to the description of Corporal Trim courting Mrs. Bridget (figs. 3.6 and 3.7).[27] In both cases, as well as in many others, a general principle is at work, which is spelled out, in a different mood, in one of Yorick's sermons: "Give but the outline of a story,—let *spleen* or *prudery* snatch the pencil, and they will finish it with so many hard strokes, and with so dirty a colouring, that *candour* and *courtesy* will fit in torture as they look at it."[28] The reader is actively involved in the production of the text, effectively counterbalancing the despotic capriciousness of the unconstrained narrator.[29]

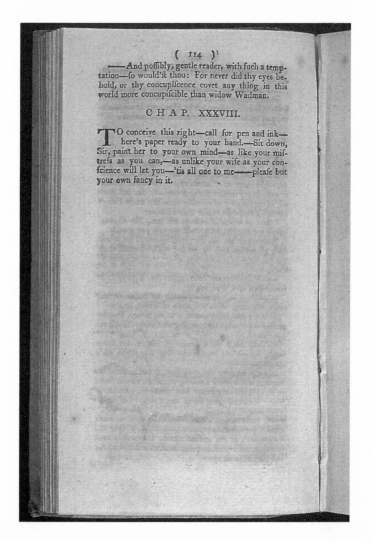

———And poffibly, gentle reader, with fuch a temp-
tation—fo would'ft thou: For never did thy eyes be-
hold, or thy concupifcence covet any thing in this
world more concupifcible than widow Wadman.

C H A P. XXXVIII.

T O conceive this right—call for pen and ink—
here's paper ready to your hand.—Sit down,
Sir, paint her to your own mind—as like your mif-
trefs as you can,—as unlike your wife as your con-
fcience will let you—'tis all one to me——pleafe but
your own fancy in it.

FIGURE 3.6. L. Sterne, *The Life and Opinions of Tristram Shandy,*
in *The Works* (London, 1779), 2:114.

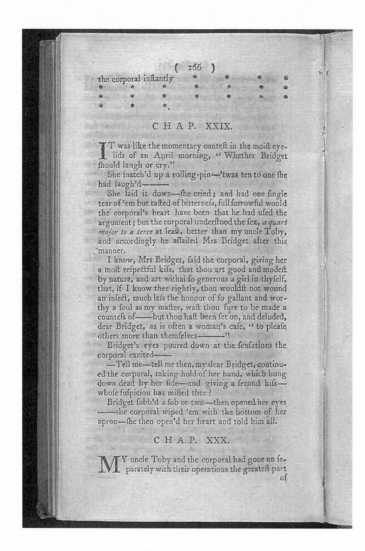

the corporal inſtantly *   *   *   *   *
*   *   *   *   *   *   *
*   *   *   *   *   *   *
*   *   *.

C H A P. XXIX.

IT was like the momentary conteſt in the moiſt eye-
lids of an April morning, "Whether Bridget
ſhould laugh or cry."

She ſnatch'd up a rolling-pin—'twas ten to one ſhe
had laugh'd———

She laid it down—ſhe cried; and had one ſingle
tear of 'em but taſted of bitterneſs, full ſorrowful would
the corporal's heart have been that he had uſed the
argument; but the corporal underſtood the ſex, *a quart
major to a terce* at leaſt, better than my uncle Toby,
and accordingly he aſſailed Mrs Bridget after this
manner.

I know, Mrs Bridget, ſaid the corporal, giving her
a moſt reſpectful kiſs, that thou art good and modeſt
by nature, and art withal ſo generous a girl in thyſelf,
that, if I know thee rightly, thou wouldſt not wound
an inſect, much leſs the honour of ſo gallant and worthy a ſoul as my maſter, waſt thou ſure to be made a
counteſs of——but thou haſt been ſet on, and deluded,
dear Bridget, as is often a woman's caſe, "to pleaſe
others more than themſelves———"

Bridget's eyes poured down at the ſenſations the
corporal excited——

—Tell me—tell me then, my dear Bridget, continued the corporal, taking hold of her hand, which hung
down dead by her ſide—and giving a ſecond kiſs—
whoſe ſuſpicion has miſled thee?

Bridget ſobb'd a ſob or two—then opened her eyes
——the corporal wiped 'em with the bottom of her
apron—ſhe then open'd her heart and told him all.

C H A P. XXX.

MY uncle Toby and the corporal had gone on ſe-
parately with their operations the greateſt part
of

FIGURE 3.7. L. Sterne, *The Life and Opinions of Tristram Shandy*, in *The Works* (London, 1779), 2:266.

7

The relationship between narrator and reader is at the very center of Sterne's handling of time in *Tristram Shandy*, possibly the most debated feature in the whole novel.[30] The gap between the reader's experience of time and the fictional time staged by the narrator reaches a climax in the following oft-quoted passage:

> I am this month one whole year older than I was this time twelve-month; and having got, as you perceive, almost into the middle of my fourth volume—and no farther than to my first day's life—'tis demonstrative that I have three hundred and sixty-four days more life to write just now, than when I first set out; so that instead of advancing, as a common writer, in my work with what I have been doing at it—on the contrary, I am just thrown so many volumes back—was every day of my life to be as busy a day as this—And why not?—and the transactions and opinions of it to take up as much description—And for what reason should they be cut short? as at this rate I should just live 364 times faster than I should write—It must follow, an' please your worships, that the more I write, the more I shall have to write—and consequently, the more your worships read, the more your worships will have to read.[31]

This extraordinary passage—"a *reductio ad absurdum* of the novel form itself," as Ian Watt labeled it[32]—translated the famous argument about Achilles and the tortoise into the relationship between narrator and reader. The argument, as we learn from Aristotle, had been put forward by Zeno of Elea. Once again, we come across Bayle, whose entry on "Zeno of Elea" is one of the most philosophically dense in the whole *Dictionary*. Incidentally, I wonder whether the anecdote (rejected by Bayle as apocryphal at the end of the entry "Zeno"), according to which Diogenes

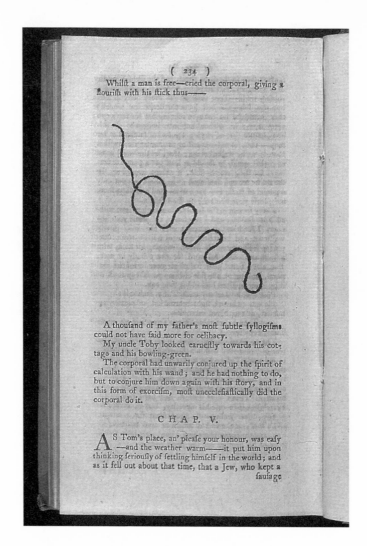

FIGURE 3.8. L. Sterne, *The Life and Opinions of Tristram Shandy*, in *The Works* (London, 1779), 2:234.

the Cynic would have refuted the subtle reasonings denying motion by the single gesture of walking, might not have inspired the famous episode of Corporal Trim shouting "Whilst a man is free" and "giving a flourish with his stick like this" (fig. 3.8). This is immediately followed by the comment "A thousand of my father's most subtle syllogisms could not have said more for celibacy."[33]

Both the implications and the difficulties of Zeno's argument are extensively discussed in remark F, which, as Bayle noticed, could be regarded as a supplement to another entry in the *Dictionary*, on "Pyrrho." But before quoting a passage from the latter, I would like to make a digression myself.

8

"In recent scholarship," remarked Ian Watt some years ago, "we can find abundant support for seeing *Tristram Shandy* as the most inclusive literary expression of a movement whose greatest philosophical representative is David Hume."[34] But to my knowledge nobody ever claimed that Hume's work had a direct impact on Sterne's before the two men met in Paris in 1764. In fact, the similarities in their respective approaches can be explained as parallel responses to a common intellectual stimulus: Bayle's *Dictionary*.

The encounter between the young Hume and Bayle's work on the "high road to Pyrrhonism," to use the title of a collection of essays by Richard Popkin, is considered today a crucial event in the history of European thought.[35] Fifty years ago, in his pioneering work, Norman Kemp Smith focused above all on the role played by Bayle, especially through the *Dictionary*'s entry on "Zeno of Elea," in influencing Hume's ideas about space and time.[36] But the related entry on "Pyrrho," remark B, may further illuminate Hume's use of Bayle. Bayle, relying on a literary device he was especially fond of, staged an alleged dialogue between

two abbots, one whereof had but common learning, the other was
a good Philosopher. . . . The first had said, somewhat coldly, that he
forgave the Heathen Philosophers, their floating in the uncertainty
of their opinions; but that he could not apprehend how there
could be any Pyrrhonists under the light of the Gospel. To which
the other answered, You are in the wrong to reason in such a manner. If Arcesilaus should return into the world, and was to dispute
with our Divines, he would be a thousand times more formidable
than he was to the Dogmatists of old Greece: the Christian Theology would afford him unanswerable arguments.[37]

At first sight, the meaning of the passage is clear. By pointing at the
weakness of Christian theology in answering the arguments of the
skeptic tradition, Bayle emphasizes the inability of human reason to
penetrate the mysteries of faith.[38] But one could also read the passage
from a different perspective: Christian theology, by fueling the Greek
and Roman skeptic tradition, made it much more far-reaching and rad-
ical. If I am not mistaken, Hume indirectly put forward this argument in
the section of his *Treatise* dealing with moral obligation: "I shall farther
observe," Hume writes, "that since every new promise imposes a new
obligation of morality on the person who promises, and since this new
obligation arises from his will; 'tis one of the most mysterious and in-
comprehensible operations that can possibly be imagin'd, and may
even be compar'd to *transubstantiation*, or *holy orders*, where a certain form
of words, along with a certain intention, changes entirely the nature of
an external object, and even of a human creature."

Hume immediately stresses the limits of his rather unexpected comparison. Far from suggesting that moral obligations and Catholic sacraments have a common origin, he stresses the opposite: "But tho' these
mysteries be so far alike, 'tis very remarkable, that they differ widely in
other particulars, and that this difference may be regarded as a strong

proof of the difference of their origins. As the obligation of promises is an invention for the interest of society, 'tis warp'd into as many different forms as that interest requires, and even runs into direct contradictions, rather than lose sight of its object."

In the case of Catholic sacraments, Hume explains, the lack of a social purpose allows them to operate according to their inner logic: "But as those other monstrous doctrines are merely priestly inventions, and have no public interest in view, they are less disturb'd in their progress by new obstacles; and it must be own'd, that, after the first absurdity, they follow more directly the current of reason and good sense. Theologians clearly perceiv'd, that the external form of words, being mere sound, require an intention to make them have any efficacy."[39]

Christian theology as a privileged ground for thought experiments: this was exactly Bayle's attitude, as the aforementioned dialogue between the two abbots shows. The philosophically trained abbot had no difficulty in proving that the mysteries of Christian religion—such as the Catholic doctrine of transubstantiation or the Trinity—were much more vulnerable to the skeptics' attacks:

> It is evident, that things which do not differ from a third, do not differ from each other, it is the basis of all our reasonings, all our syllogisms are grounded upon it: nevertheless we are assured by the revelation of the mystery of the Trinity, that this is a false axiom. . . . It is evident, that there is no difference between *individuum*, *nature*, and *person*: nevertheless, the same mystery has convinced us, that persons may be multiplied and that individuums and natures will not cease for all that to be one. . . . It is evident, that a human body cannot be in several places at one time, and that its head cannot be penetrated, with all its others points, under an indivisible point: nevertheless the mystery of the Eucharist teaches us, that these two things happen every day, from whence

it follows, that neither you nor I can be sure whether we are distinguished from other men, and whether we are not at this very moment in the seraglio of Constantinople, in Canada, and in Japan, and in every town of the world, under several circumstances in each place.[40]

9

Let us go back to *Tristram Shandy*. In one of his most extraordinary self-reflecting meditations Sterne once again translated Bayle's thought experiment based on the Trinity into fictional terms:

In this last chapter, as far at least as it has helped me through Auxerre, I have been getting forwards in two different journeys together, and with the same dash of the pen—for I have got entirely out of Auxerre in this journey which I am writing now, and I am got half way out of Auxerre in that which I shall write hereafter—There is but a certain degree of perfection in every thing; and by pushing at something beyond that, I have brought myself into such a situation, as no traveller ever stood before me; for I am this moment walking across the market-place of Auxerre with my father and my uncle Toby, in our way back to dinner—and I am this moment also entering Lyons with my post-chaise broke into a thousand pieces—and I am moreover this moment in a handsome pavillion built by Pringello, upon the banks of the Garonne, which Mons. Sligniac has lent me, and where I now sit rhapsodizing all these affairs.

—Let me collect myself, and pursue my journey.[41]

One is reminded of Hume's famous definition of the self: "nothing but a bundle or collection of different perceptions, which succeed each other with an inconceivable rapidity, and are in a perpetual flux and movement."[42] But was not Hume also reacting to Bayle? As I suggested before, Bayle's paradoxes based on the definition of person in the dogma of the Trinity might have played an important role in the development of Hume's critique of personal identity. I even wonder whether Hume's epoch-making conclusion that "all the nice and subtle questions concerning personal identity can never possibly be decided, and are to be regarded rather as grammatical than as philosophical difficulties" could not be an echo of Bayle's approach to some crucial Christian dogmas.[43] The debate on the relationship between Christ's human and divine nature, settled in the council of Ephesus in 431, was simply a matter of words, Bayle wrote in the entry on "Nestorius" in his *Dictionary*. Cyrillus, who condemned Nestorius as a heretic for having rejected the so-called hypostatic union of the two natures in the person of Christ, might have spared the church, Bayle goes on, a lot of trouble: "There needed nothing more than to give reciprocally a just definition of their terms."[44]

An echo of this complaint can be heard in another passage of Sterne's novel:

What a pudder and racket in COUNCILS about οὐσία and ὑπόστασις; and in the SCHOOLS of the learned about power and about spirit;—about essences and about quintessences;—about substances, and about space.—What confusion in greater THEATRES from words of little meaning, and as indeterminate a sense;—when thou consider this, thou wilt not wonder at my uncle Toby's perplexities,—thou wilt drop a tear of pity upon his scarp and his counterscarp;—his glacis and his covered way;—his ravelin and his half-moon: 'Twas not by ideas,—by heaven! his life was put in jeopardy by words.[45]

But the narrator is well aware that the use of simpler words would not be enough to clarify the intricate relationship between words and reality. Even the most innocent questions can become highly problematic, as the splendid exchange between the French commissary and Tristram shows:

My good friend, quoth I—as sure as I am I—and you are you—
—And who are you? said he.—Don't puzzle me; said I.[46]

The last remark, as has been noticed, has a definite Humean flavor. But I wonder whether Tristram's puzzlement might not conceal also an allusion to another, albeit repressed answer to the commissary's question, an answer that would have replicated the previous tautology—"as sure as I am I"—by saying "I am that I am."

I cannot prove this hypothetical allusion to Exodus 3:14. But I hope to have proved that Bayle and his theological concerns throw some light on the paradoxically split personality who says "I" in *Tristram Shandy*, as well as on the peculiar structure of the novel.

CHAPTER FOUR

Tusitala and His Polish Reader

1

ROBERT LOUIS STEVENSON started using the pseudonym Tusitala—a Samoan word meaning, approximately, "Storyteller"—in the spring of 1892.[1] A few months earlier, his short story "The Bottle Imp," first issued in the Sunday *New York Herald* between February 8 and March 1, 1891, had been translated into Samoan and published in the missionary magazine *O Le Sulu Samoa* (The Samoan torch). This was the first instance of a printed text in the Samoan language. Stevenson had worked on the translation with A. E. Claxton, a local missionary.[2]

In December 1892, in a letter addressed to Sidney Colvin, his long-time friend and publisher, Stevenson wrote that "The Bottle Imp" should be seen as "the centre piece" of his forthcoming collection *Island Nights' Entertainments*: "You always had an idea that I depreciated the 'B[ottle]. I[mp]'; I can't think wherefore; I always particularly liked it—one of my best works, and ill to equal."[3]

To clarify some of the possible reasons for Stevenson's high evaluation of "The Bottle Imp," it is useful to reinsert this short piece into a larger context.

2

Although "The Bottle Imp" is deservedly well known, it makes sense to start with a résumé of its plot. A young sailor from Hawaii, named

Keawe, is taking a walk along the streets of San Francisco. He sees a beautiful house and conceives a longing to own one like it. A sad-looking man, who turns out to be the owner of the house, enters into conversation with Keawe and soon informs him that his wishes will be fulfilled if only he buys from him a marvelous bottle. Inside the bottle, he is told, is an imp capable of granting the owner of the bottle his every request, except the wish for a longer life. The bottle "cannot be sold at all, unless sold at a loss," otherwise it will unfailingly be returned to the hands of he who violates this rule. "If a man dies before he sells it, he must burn in hell for ever." Long before the price of the bottle had been extremely high; it is now being sold quite cheaply.

After some uncertainty Keawe pays all the money he has—fifty dollars—and takes the bottle. Through a series of unforeseeable circumstances he becomes the owner of a beautiful house in Hawaii. He gets rid of the bottle, selling it to a friend for forty-nine dollars, and lives happily for some time. Then he meets a girl, Kokua, and falls in love with her; he would like to marry her but discovers that he had contracted leprosy. In order to recover his health Keawe tries to regain possession of the bottle. He goes to Honolulu, follows the traces of the gifts of the little imp, and finds the latest owner. But in the meantime the price of the bottle has fallen so precipitously that it costs only two cents. Keawe buys the bottle, returns to Hawaii, and marries Kokua. But his heart is broken, because he knows that he will be damned. Kokua, however, is ready to fight: "What is this you say about a cent? But all the world is not American. In England they have a piece they call a farthing, which is about half a cent. Ah! sorrow!" she cries, "that makes it scarcely better, for the buyer must be lost, and we shall find none so brave as my Keawe! But, then, there is France: they have a small coin there which they call a centime, and these go five to the cent, or thereabout. We could not do better. Come, Keawe, let us go to the French islands; let us go to Tahiti as fast as ships can bear us. There we have four centimes, three centimes, two centimes, one centime; four possible sales to come and go on; and two of us to push the bargain."

The last words anticipate the developments of the plot: since they are unable to find other buyers, man and wife heroically deceive each other, arranging transactions through two intermediaries, in order to rescue the loved one from hell. But the last intermediary—a drunkard—decides to keep the miraculous bottle for himself. He will burn in hell, and the couple will be happy.

3

When it first appeared in the Sunday *New York Herald*, "The Bottle Imp" was introduced by the following note: "Any student of that very unliterary product, the English drama of the early part of the century, will here recognise the name and the root idea of a piece once rendered popular by the redoubtable O. Smith. The root idea is there, and identical, and yet I hope I have made it a new thing. And the fact that the tale has been designed and written for a Polynesian audience may lend it some extraneous interest nearer home."[4]

In preparing for publication his collection entitled *Island Nights' Entertainments*, Stevenson asked Sidney Colvin to get rid of this note and set in its place a subtitle: "The Bottle Imp: A Cue from an Old Melodrama." Colvin suppressed the subtitle and kept the note.[5] In some recent editions the note has disappeared.[6] But long ago erudites succeeded in identifying the sources of Stevenson's story. Ultimately, the plot goes back to two motifs from German folklore: one is the "Galgenmännlein," a little man born from the sperm of a hanged person, and the other is the magic bottle that can be sold only at a lower price. Both motifs had already been combined in Grimmelshausen's *Trutz Simplex*, published in 1670, which also included the search for a less valuable coin in another land.[7] Through a series of literary intermediaries the plot came to England. The "old melodrama" mentioned by Stevenson has been identified as *The Bottle Imp: A Melo-dramatic Romance in Two Acts*, written by R. B. Peake and produced at the Theatre Royal, English Opera House, in July 1828; it was printed from a stage copy. I have consulted an edition published that was ten years later.[8] The play involved a series of colorful characters, including a Jew named Shadrack, provided with "broad trimmed Jew's hat with red crown, brown jacket and trunks, black stockings." In the last scene Nicola, the hero, screams: "I can again sell thee, fiend!" The curtain falls down as the imp inexorably responds: "No, the coin with which thou have repurchased me is of the lowest value in the world."

Stevenson's "redoubtable O. Smith" who used to play the imp, was in fact the actor Richard John Smith, who died in 1855.[9] Stevenson was then five years old. According to a contemporary description, Smith wore a "tightly-fitting skin dress of a sea green, horns on the head, and demon's face, from the wrist to the hips a wide-spreading wing, extending or folding at pleasure."[10] The germ of Stevenson's "Bottle Imp" may well have been a childhood recollection.

During the last decades "that very unliterary product, the English drama of the early part of the century," has become at last a region of literary history unto itself. In a remarkable book Peter Brooks explored the impact of French melodrama and "the mode of excess" on Balzac and Henry James.[11] The English melodrama, which addressed itself to a more popular audience, could also, as Stevenson's "The Bottle Imp" shows, produce sophisticated literary offspring. Stevenson claimed to have transformed the "Bottle Imp root idea" into "a new thing . . . designed and written for a Polynesian audience." The transformations required by this new audience were not too extensive, since the original story turned around the magical helper: a very widespread—in fact, transcultural—motif, with which we are familiar thanks to Vladimir Propp's great book *Morphology of the Folk-Tale*.[12]

In a footnote to his essay on the sources of "The Bottle Imp," J. W. Beach mentioned Cazotte's *Diable boiteux*, Balzac's *Peau de chagrin*, and the imprisoned djinn of the Arabian Nights, concluding that "these do not take us far."[13] On the contrary, a comparison with Balzac's *Peau de chagrin* seems to throw some interesting light on Stevenson's short story.

4

La Peau de chagrin (*The Wild Ass's Skin*) was first published in 1831. Goethe, then in his eighties, read it with admiration, a response not devoid of narcissism, since Balzac's novel had clearly been inspired by *Faust*.[14] But both devil and damnation are absent from the plot of *La Peau de chagrin*. The novel's hero, Raphaël de Valentin, obtains unlimited power through the wild ass's skin but the price is his life, not his soul. In France, Goethe's *Faust* had been transformed first into a pantomime and then into a melodrama; Balzac's reworking of the Faust motif was consistent with the spirit of the latter, a genre in which supernatural elements were framed by a secular context.[15] This contrast is a major theme in Balzac's novel. When Raphaël comes across the mysterious old man who is the previous owner of the wild ass's skin, the narrator remarks: "This scene took place in Paris, on the Quai Voltaire, in the nineteenth century, at a time and place which should surely rule out the possibility of magic."[16]

The allusion to Voltaire's house—"the house in which the apostle of French skepticism had breathed his last"—is immediately contrasted with the symbol of the present age: Raphaël is "perturbed by the inexplicable feeling of being confronted by some strange power, an emotion similar to that we have all felt in the presence of Napoleon."[17] Later, faced with the magical shrinking of the wild ass's skin, which announces the shrinking of his remaining time among the living, Raphaël shouts in indignation: "What! . . . In a century of enlightenment during which we have learned that diamonds are carbon crystals, in an age when there is an explanation for everything, when the police would haul a new Messiah before the courts and refer his miracles to the

Academy of Sciences, at a time when we require a notary's initials before trusting anything, why should I alone believe in a sort of *Mene, Mene,
Tekel, Parsin?* . . . Let us consult the scientists."[18]

But even the scientists—a zoologist, a physicist, a chemist—prove in-
capable of preventing the shrinking of the wild ass's skin. Their defeat
has a larger, symbolic meaning. In a letter to Charles de Montalembert,
the Catholic writer, Balzac wrote that *The Wild Ass's Skin* was "the formu-
la of human life, if one disregards all individual features . . . there all is
myth and figure" (tout y est mythe et figure).[19] The novel is introduced
by the sign traced in the air by *Tristram Shandy*'s Corporal Trim, chosen by
Balzac as a motto to signify "les ondulations bizarres de la destinée,"
"destiny's bizarre vicissitudes" (fig. 4.1), which was meant to emphasize
the power of irrational forces on individuals and society, a point at the
core of the *Comédie humaine* as a whole.[20] "How can one traverse such a

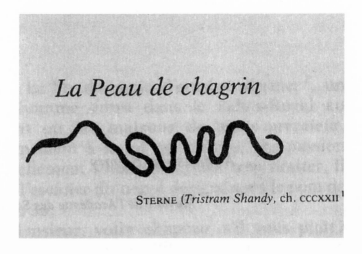

La Peau de chagrin

STERNE (*Tristram Shandy*, ch. CCCXXII[1]

FIGURE 4.1. A page of H. de Balzac's *La peau de chagrin*.

fresco," Balzac once wrote, "without the resources of the Arabian tale, without the aid of buried titans? In the tempest that has raged for half a century, controlling the waves there are giants hidden under the boards of the social third underground."[21] In order to provide an adequate description of the forces at work in modern society, one has to tap, according to Balzac, "the resources of the Arabian tale," using "myths" and "figures" like the wild ass's skin.

As is well known, both Karl Marx and Friedrich Engels were great admirers of Balzac. According to Paul Lafargue, his son-in law, Marx even planned to write an article on Balzac, which he was postponing until after the (never achieved) completion of *Capital*.[22] On several occasions Marx and Engels praised Balzac's extraordinary gift for social observation. But Marx also responded to the visionary side of Balzac's oeuvre.[23] In a famous sentence from *The Eighteenth Brumaire*, "The tradition of all generations weighs like a nightmare [*ein Alp*] on the brain of the living," a perceptive scholar has detected the echo of a passage from Balzac's *Colonel Chabert*: "The social and judicial world weighed on his breast like a nightmare."[24] Balzac's powerful metaphor of the wild ass's skin might have contributed to the *Capital* chapter "The Fetishism of Commodities and Its Secret," which stresses the mystical side of commodities "with its metaphysical subtleties and theological niceties," as well as, more generally, the role of irrational elements in capitalist society.[25]

5

Stevenson presumably never read Marx, but he did read Balzac. In his early twenties he sent to his friend Charles Baxter an imitation of Balzac's *Contes Drolatiques*.[26] A writer's parody of another writer is always instructive, as Marcel Proust's different versions of *L'affaire Lemoine* (an admittedly special case) show.[27] Stevenson's complex attitude toward Balzac emerges from a splendid letter addressed in 1883 to Bob Stevenson, his cousin:

Were you to re-read some Balzac, as I have been doing, it would greatly help to clear your eyes. He was a man who never found his method. An inarticulate Shakespeare, smothered under forcible—feeble detail. It is astounding, to the riper mind, how bad he is, how feeble, how untrue, how tedious; and of course, when he surrendered to his temperament, how good and powerful. And yet never plain nor clear. He could not consent to the dull, and thus became so. He would leave nothing undeveloped, and thus drowned out of sight of land amid the multitude of crying and incongruous details. Jesus, there is but one art: to omit! O if I knew how to omit, I would ask no other knowledge. A man who knew how to omit would make an *Iliad* of a daily paper.[28]

Giuseppe Tomasi di Lampedusa, the author of *Il gattopardo* (*The Leopard*), used to deliver to a circle of friends informal lectures on French and English literature; a collection of them was published after his death.[29] Lampedusa half-jokingly referred to an opposition he was particularly fond of, between "fat" and "thin" writers (in a stylistic sense). In the case of Balzac and Stevenson the opposition was both stylistic and corporeal. Balzac's luxuriant abundance of details taught Stevenson to find his own literary identity, by teaching him how "to omit." Let me give two examples of Stevenson's art of omitting, both taken from "The Bottle Imp." Keawe, the hero, before selling the bottle to his friend Lopaka, says:

"I have a curiosity myself.—So come, let us have one look at you, Mr. Imp."
Now as soon as that was said the imp looked out of the bottle, and in again, swift as a lizard; and there sat Keawe and Lopaka turned to stone. The night had quite come, before either found a thought to say or voice to say it with; and then Lopaka pushed the money over and took the bottle.

The other example occurs a little later. Keawe has received the imp's gift, his beautiful house. He is happy; he asks his Chinese servant to prepare him a bath:

> So the Chinaman had word, and he must rise from sleep, and light the furnaces; and as he wrought below, beside the boilers, he heard his master singing and rejoicing above him in the lighted chambers. When the water began to be hot the Chinaman cried to his master: and Keawe went into the bathroom; and the Chinaman heard him sing as he filled the marble basin; and heard him sing, and the singing broken, as he undressed; until of a sudden, the song ceased. The Chinaman listened, and listened; he called up the house to Keawe to ask if all were well, and Keawe answered him "Yes," and bade him go to bed; but there was no more singing in the Bright House; and all night long the Chinaman heard his master's feet go round and round the balconies without repose.

Both passages are beautifully done, although in the latter a fussy reader might perhaps wish for one more little omission, the words "as he undressed," which spoil, with their visual associations, the coherence of the strictly aural point of view (if I may say so) of the description. Furthermore, this slight infelicity is magnified unwillingly by the repetition of the same words in the next sentence: "Now, the truth of it was this: as Keawe undressed for his bath, he spied upon his flesh a patch like a patch of lichen on a rock, and it was then that he stopped singing. For he knew the likeness of that patch, and knew that he was fallen in the Chinese Evil," that is, leprosy.[30]

One can easily imagine the flow of emotional utterances that would have been generated in a Balzac novel by, respectively, the appearance of the imp and the discovery of the hero's leprosy. But because Stevenson's literary imperative was restraint, he regarded Balzac as a challenge. "The Bottle Imp" shares with *The Wild Ass's Skin* a starting point—the magical helper motif—but its decor and plot are utterly different. Stevenson's imagination, I would argue, had been sparked by a specific passage in Balzac's novel, the moment when the mysterious old man gives the wild ass's skin to Raphaël: "Then he began again thus: 'Without forcing you to beg, without causing you to blush, without giving you a French centime, a Levantine para, a German heller, a Russian kopek, a Scottish farthing, a single sestertium or obol of the ancient world or a piastre of the new world, without offering you anything whatsoever in gold, silver, bullion, banknotes or letter of credit, I will make you richer, more powerful and more respected than a king can be—in a constitutional monarchy.' "[31]

This cumulative list—a device Balzac was particularly fond of—means that the old man is not asking for money, not even the smallest coin in the world. But the mention of the German heller and the Scottish farthing must have brought back to Stevenson's mind the story of the Bottle Imp. The hero of one version, published in *Popular Tales and Romances of the Northern Nations*, pays a heller for the bottle. After that, "the thing of the utmost consequence for him now to do, was to enquire every where for some coin of less value than a heller"; therefore he was nicknamed "crazy Half-heller."[32] In "The Mandrake," another version of the same story included in the anthology *The German Novelists*, Reichard, the hero, finally succeeds in selling the imp for one "base farthing."[33] Stevenson, who in his own retelling of the story mentioned both farthing and centime, omitted the Faust motif, which is conspicuously present in most Bottle Imp versions, including the one performed by the "redoubtable O. Smith." Stevenson pushed to the forefront instead the idea that the magical object had to be exchanged along a monetary—although antiprofit—circuit—stretched along an enormous sea distance: from San Francisco, to the Hawaii Islands, to Tahiti.

6

Stevenson's "The Bottle Imp" was first published in 1891. Twenty-five

years later and several thousand miles westward, Bronislaw Malinowski, a Polish-born anthropologist based in England, although still a subject of the Austro-Hungarian empire, started his fieldwork in the Trobriand islands. This stage of Malinowski's life, momentous both for him
and for the discipline he helped to transform, can be followed nearly
day by day—some long interruptions notwithstanding—through a double lens: his diaries and his correspondence with Elsie Masson, then his
fiancée and later his wife.[34] The former source is highly controversial,
on many levels. Malinowski's diaries, published in 1967 under the edito-
rial title of *A Diary in the Strict Sense of the Term*, were never intended for
publication. Most commentators reacted with shock and dismay to Malinowski's blatantly racist attitude toward the Trobriand natives. One re-
viewer, I. M. Lewis, noticed with some surprise that in the diaries there
is "little theorising about field data or techniques. . . . There are highly
condensed and elliptical theoretical and methodological points noted
from time to time, but these are usually so cryptic that they are difficult
to follow let alone evaluate."[35] My inquiry will focus precisely on some
of those cryptic passages.

The diaries cover two distinct periods of Malinowski's fieldwork: the
first, between early September 1914 and early August 1915, on Mailu Island; the second, between the end of October 1917 and mid-July 1918,
first on Samarai and then in the Trobriand Islands. Only one entry, a few
lines long, is related to his first trip to the Trobriands.

The tone of the two diaries is markedly different. The first is filled with
lyrical descriptions of landscapes into which Malinowski projected different feelings, from sexual desire to metaphysical reflections. At the end
of the sea journey from Mailu, his first fieldwork experience, Malinowski
wrote under the date March 4, 1914 (he was then entering his thirtieth
year), the following remarks: "Should like to make a synthesis of this voyage. Actually the marvelous sights filled me with a noncreative delight. As
I gazed, everything echoed inside me, as when listening to music. More-

over I was full of plans for the future.—The sea is blue, absorbing every-thing, fused with the sky. At moments, the pink silhouettes of the moun-tains appear through the mist, like phantoms of reality in the flood of blue, like the unfinished ideas of some youthful creative force."[36]

This is the voice of a young man, on the brink of his shadow line (the reference to Conrad is, for many reasons, unavoidable). In the second diary the landscape descriptions are more laconic; the tone is often matter-of-fact; the "unfinished ideas" are now pretty focused, the "youthful creative force" has acquired a definite direction. Malinowski is intensely working on his ethnographic project, which had crystallized around a topic: the *kula*. In a preliminary article, published in *Man* in July 1920, Malinowski defined the kula as a special trading system, stretched over an enormous geographical area—which he labeled "the Kula ring"—based on "two articles of high value, but of no real use . . . arm-shells . . . and necklets of red shell-discs" and involving a series of high-ly complex rituals.[37] *Kula: A Tale of Native Enterprise and Adventure in the South Seas*, one of the titles suggested by Malinowski, ultimately became, in 1922, *Argonauts of the Western Pacific*.[38]

Before Malinowski, the kula had barely been mentioned in the an-thropological literature.[39] It is unclear when he came to realize the im-portance of his discovery.[40] As he recalled in his book, Malinowski had first witnessed a kula transaction, without realizing what was going on, in February 1915 on his way back to Australia, at the end of his first expedi-tion to New Guinea.[41] During the full year he spent in the Trobriand Is-lands, between May 1915 and May 1916, Malinowski collected evidence about the kula and planned to write an article on it. But a letter he wrote to Elsie from Samarai on November 10, 1917, reveals a depressed mood, as if he were still looking for a way to accomplish this: "I expect the kula article will remain unfinished, till I return. . . . Moreover, it seems so ab-surd to write things about the *kula*, when any nigger walking about the street in a dirty Lavalava might know much more about it than I do!"[42]

On this point Malinowski completely changed his mind. Consider this eloquent passage from *Argonauts of the Western Pacific*, which sounds like a theoretical manifesto:

> The Kula is thus an extremely big and complex institution, both in its geographical extent, and in the manifoldness of its component pursuits. . . . Yet it must be remembered that what appears to us as an extensive, complicated, and yet well ordered institution is the outcome of ever so many doings and pursuits, carried on by savages, who have no laws or aims or charters definitely laid down. They have no knowledge of the *total outline* of any of their social structure. . . . Not even the most intelligent native has any clear idea of the Kula as a big, organized social construction, still less of its sociological function and implications. If you were to ask him what the Kula is, he would answer by giving a few details, most likely by giving his personal experiences and subjective views on the Kula, but nothing approaching the definition just given here. . . . For the integral picture does not exist in his mind; he is in it, and cannot see the whole from the outside.
>
> The integration of all the details observed, the achievement of a sociological synthesis of all the various, relevant symptoms is the task of the Ethnographer. First of all, he has to find out that certain activities, which at first sight might appear incoherent and not correlated, have a meaning. . . . The Ethnographer has to *construct* the picture of the big institution, very much as the physicist constructs his theory from the experimental data, which always have been within reach of everybody, but which needed a consistent interpretation.[43]

These remarks are hardly compatible with the old stereotype, according to which Malinowski was a keen observer and collector of data that he then framed in a rather rigid functionalist theory. It seems that the very experience of writing a diary helped him to recognize the role played by theory in making sense of scattered data, in transforming them into meaningful facts. On November 13, 1917, Malinowski wrote in his diary:

> Thoughts: writing of retrospective diary suggests many reflections: a diary is a "history" of events which are entirely accessible to the observer, and yet writing a diary requires profound knowledge and thorough training; change from theoretical point of view; experience in writing leads to entirely different results even if the observer remains the same—let alone if there are different observers! Consequently, we cannot speak of objectively existing facts: theory creates facts. Consequently there is no such thing as "history" as an independent science. History is observation of facts in keeping with a certain theory; an application of this theory to the facts as time gives birth to them.[44]

This passage reminds us not only of Malinowski's youthful essays on, respectively, Nietzsche and Mach but more generally of the Polish intellectual tradition known above all through the belated impact of Ludwik Fleck's book about the Wassermann reaction, *Genesis and Development of a Scientific Fact*, on Thomas Kuhn's *The Structure of Scientific Revolutions*, published twenty-five years later. The title of Fleck's book is in itself significant.[45] "Theory creates facts"; the ethnographer has to construct the kula "very much as the physicist constructs his theory from the experimental data," as Malinowski wrote, respectively, in his diary and in his book. How did he succeed in constructing a theory that put the scattered data he had collected about the kula into a meaningful configuration?

7

On October 26, 1917, Elsie Masson wrote to her fiancé: "I shall get you Stevenson's letters to dabble into. His type of thought may strike you as childish, but I think you cannot fail to like his personality. He was so un-wowserish, so genuine, weak in many ways but so likeable, and then you must be interested in his struggle with ill-health."[46]

Malinowski received Stevenson's letters—they must have been the *Vailima Letters*, edited by Sidney Colvin—two months later, in mid-December. Elsie's guesses about her fiancé's reactions were not off the mark. On December 23, 1917, Malinowski wrote to her:

I have read a good deal of Stevenson's letters. You were quite right, I am quite fascinated by them, at least partially. Stevenson's egotistic interest in his health and his work is, alas, so damnably like my own case that I cannot help finding passages which I almost have said myself. . . R.L.S.'s egotism strikes even me as too Slavonic and too effeminate at times. But I am afraid my letters would show exactly the same note. I was very much struck by a passage in which he sings the praise of his enduring, patient heroism in the continuous struggle with ill health and in his striving to do the work in spite of sickness and depression and failing forces. I felt like that myself so often and indeed had I not felt this note of heroism in this ignoble battle, when the weapons are a syringe . . . tabloids and solutions, it would have been impossible to go on. . . . There may be spontaneous virtue and an easy flow of creative power, coming from a super-abundance of strength. But the tragic case of an ambitious and gifted man, who has got his invaluable burden to carry and to lay down at a certain spot, and who lacks the brute physical force to do it, is as worthy of regard as the other, and I am afraid it leads invariably to this keen interest in oneself, to this extreme self consciousness in appreciating every achievement and the tendency to dwell on it and to tell it to all one's friends. . . .
It was funny also to read here, on the shores of the lagoon and under the coconuts, S's descriptions of Samoa and Honolulu and

his intense and selfconscious appreciation of the exotic strangeness of his new existence in the light of the litterary milieu of civilized London, in which Colvin was living. I also very keenly and
self-consciously feel this contrast and strangeness.[47]

Malinowski's striking self-identification has been overshadowed by
the now-famous remark he made a few years later in a letter to Bren-
da Seligman: "[W. H. R.] Rivers is the Rider Haggard of anthropology; I
shall be the Conrad." Malinowski was obviously deeply impressed by
Conrad's work, although he wrote in his diary that he had finished *The
Secret Agent* "with a feeling of disgust."[48] But on a personal level, through
his health problems (and his health obsessions as well), Malinowski felt
much closer to Stevenson's egotism: a closeness paradoxically emphasized by the label "too Slavonic and too effeminate." In Stevenson's *Vailima Letters* Malinowski found a mirror image of his own situation: a highly civilized individual being confronted with "the exotic strangeness of
his new existence." Some glimpses of this existence, such as a ceremo-
nial distribution of food gifts, which Stevenson described with a great
abundance of ethnographic detail, must have deeply intrigued Malinowski, who was then trying to make sense of the role of gifts in the
Trobriand Islands. In leafing through the *Vailima Letters* Malinowski may
have also come across the letter in which Stevenson informed Colvin
of the forthcoming translation of "The Bottle Imp" into Samoan.[49] Was
Malinowski already familiar with Stevenson's short story? And if not,
did he try to satisfy a curiosity likely to be piqued by a piece that, as
Colvin noted in a footnote, had been read "with wonder and delight" by
many Samoan readers?

These questions are not preposterous, since Malinowski, an incredi-
bly voracious reader, had brought from Melbourne a considerable provision of books, occasionally supplemented by his European acquaintances living in the Trobriand Islands. In the years covered by his diaries

Malinowski read Machiavelli and the *Golden Legend*, Racine and Kipling, George Meredith and Victor Hugo, and so forth, along with a lot of trashy novels, which he used to devour with a great deal of guilt (in his diaries he repeatedly mentioned lecherous thoughts and these novels as temptations from which he should absolutely refrain).[50] Reading "The Bottle Imp" afresh or recalling its plot Malinowski would have been confronted with a fictional representation focusing on a monetary, antiprofit exchange, connected to some definite symbolic constraints, that allowed the circulation of a highly valued object through a series of islands stretched over a vast expanse of ocean. There is no need to emphasize the analogy between this representation and the ethnographer's global image of the kula, so different from the partial perception shared by the native actors involved in it. Stevenson's short story would have given Malinowski not the actual content of his discovery of course but the ability to see it, through a leap of imagination, as a whole, as a gestalt, to construct it, as he wrote later, "very much as the physicist constructs his theory from the experimental data."

I have no evidence that Malinowski read "The Bottle Imp." But on December 21, 1917, five days after the arrival of Stevenson's letters, Malinowski wrote the following entry in his diary:

> Woke up around 4 very tired. I thought of a passage from [R. L.] Stevenson's letters in which he speaks of a heroic struggle against illness and exhaustion. . . . All that day longing for civilization. I thought about friends in Melbourne. At night in the dinghy, pleasantly ambitious thoughts: I'll surely be an "eminent Polish scholar." This will be my last ethnological escapade. After that, I'll devote myself to constructive sociology: methodology, political economy, etc., and in Poland I can realize my ambitions better than anywhere else.—Strong contrast between my dreams of a civilized life and my life with the savages. I resolve to eliminate the elements (com-

ponents) of laziness and sloth from my present life. Don't read
novels unless this is necessary. Try *not* to forget creative ideas.

(pp. 160–61)

What strikes me in this passage is not so much Malinowski's fantasy
involving recognition as a scholar (he had dreamed about this before)[51]
as his allusion, unprecedented in the diaries, to "creative ideas" that were
just beginning to emerge. A few months later these ideas had apparently taken a more definite form. In an entry dated March 6, 1918, Malinowski asked himself whether his hypotheses might affect his collect-
ing of ethnographic data, an issue that, significantly, he had never
mentioned before: "New theoretical point. (1) Definition of a given cere-
mony, spontaneously formulated by the Negroes. (2) Definition arrived
at after they have been 'pumped' by *leading questions*. (3) Definition arrived
at by interpretation of concrete data" (p. 217).

A few weeks later a breakthrough occurred. Later still, on April 20,
Malinowski was to refer to it retrospectively, speaking of his "joy at Nu'a-
gasi, when suddenly *the veil was rent*" (p. 257; italics in original).[52] The entry
dated March 25 conveys the event's immediacy: "Came back at 12:30 —
the Nu'agasi were just leaving — I could not even photograph them. Fa-
tigue. Lay down — closed my mind, and at this moment revelations:
spiritual purity." A passage in inverted commas follows, printed in italics.
According to the rules set by Norbert Guterman, the *Diary*'s editor and
translator, it must have been written in a language different from Polish,
possibly English: "*Heed kindly other people's souls, but don't bury yourself in them.
If they are pure, then they reflect the world's everlasting Beauty, and then why look at
the mirrored picture if you can see the thing itself face to face? Or else they are full of
the tangled [woof] of petty intrigue and of that it is better to know nothing.*"[53]

This apparent quotation, which I have been unable to identify, brings
to the surface the religious connotations of Malinowski's "revelations,"
wrapping them in a mixture of Plato (the everlasting Beauty) and Saint

Paul (1 Cor 13:12). The diary entry continues with an account of how Malinowski took his dinghy and rowed around the promontory. At that very moment, we read in *Argonauts*, Malinowski understood the force of ritual surrounding the kula: "In the evening, after a busy day, as it was a full-moon night, I went for a long pull in a dinghey. Although in the Trobriands I had had accounts of the custom of the first halt, yet it gave me a surprise when on rounding a rocky point I came upon the whole crowd of Gumasila natives, who had departed on the Kula that morning, sitting in full-moon light on a beach, only a few miles from the village which they had left with so much to-do some ten hours before."[54]

The diary account was at the same time more elusive and more emotional: "Then I rowed around the promontory, the moon hidden behind lacy clouds. . . . Distinct feeling that next to this actual ocean, different every day, covered with clouds, rain, wind, *like a changing soul is covered with moods*—that beyond it there is an Absolute Ocean, which is more or less correctly marked on the map but which exists outside all maps and outside the reality accessible to [observation].—*Emotional origin of Platonic Ideas*" (pp. 234–35).

In a well-known essay Ernest Gellner labeled Malinowski "Zeno from Cracow."[55] On the basis of this crucial passage (seemingly overlooked, to my surprise, by all interpreters) I would call him instead "Plato from Cracow," a side that Malinowski carefully concealed.[56] What Malinowski saw during that momentous night was something above reality: the Platonic idea of kula, a reflex of "the world's everlasting Beauty."

"Suddenly," Malinowski wrote in his diary, "*I tumble back* into the real milieu with which I am also in contact. Then again suddenly they [the natives] stop existing *in their inner reality*, I see them as an *incongruous yet artistic and [savage], exotic=unreal, intangible, floating on the surface of reality, like a multicolored picture on the face of a solid but drab wall*."[57] A work of pure fiction like Stevenson's "The Bottle Imp" may have provided access to this "solid but drab wall."[58]

It is worthwhile recalling that in reassessing the kula sixty years after Malinowski, Edmund Leach rejected the kula ring concept, claiming that, since it is beyond the actors' perception, "it contains a large part of fiction." Leach urged "Melanasian specialists" to be "more functionalist in a Malinowskian sense. There is no such thing as THE KULA."[59] Malinowski, the disguised Platonist, would not have agreed.

8

The kula, wrote Malinowski in his *Argonauts*, refuted the assumption then current about primitive man as "a rational being who wants nothing but to satisfy his simplest needs and does it according to the economic principle of least effort" (p. 516). An additional target was the "so-called materialistic conception of history" (Malinowski was apparently unaware that Karl Marx was on his side). But the implications of Malinowski's discovery went far beyond the so-called primitive economy, as its belated offsprings show, from Marcel Mauss's essay on "The Gift," to Karl Polanyi's *Great Transformation*, to (more indirectly) E. P. Thompson's essay on moral economy.[60] What was really at stake was the notion of *homo oeconomicus*, which is still very much around. But as both Stevenson's and Malinowski's archipelagoes remind us, just as no man is an island, no island is an island.

Notes

Unless otherwise noted, translations are mine.

Introduction

1. T. W. Adorno, "The Essay as Form" (1958), *New German Critique*, no. 32 (spring–summer 1984): 151–71, especially 161.
2. Athenaeus, *Deipnosophists* ("The Sophists at Dinner"). See M. Bakhtin, "From the Prehistory of Novelistic Discourse," in *The Dialogic Imagination*, ed. M. Holquist (Austin, 1981), pp. 42–83, especially pp. 52–53.
3. J. Starobinski, "Peut-on définir l'*essai*?" in *Jean Starobinski*, Cahiers pour un temps (Paris, 1985), pp. 185–96.
4. M. de Montaigne, *Oeuvres complètes*, ed. A. Thibaudet and M. Rat (Paris, 1962), p. 1056. Cf. *The Complete Works of Montaigne*, ed. D. M. Frame (Stanford, 1958), p. 826: "In fine, all this fricassee that I am scribbling here is nothing but a record of the essays of my life."
5. Adorno, "The Essay as Form," p. 164.
6. V. Shklovsky, *La mossa del cavallo* (1923), trans. M. Olsoufieva (Bari, 1967); V. Foa, *Il cavallo e la torre* (Turin, 1991).
7. C. Ginzburg, *Clues, Myths, and the Historical Method* (Baltimore, 1989), pp. 96–128, 102–3. "A gesture worthy of a Neolithic hunter," commented Italo Calvino with an air of amusement in *La Repubblica*, January 21, 1980. See T. C. Cave, *Recognitions: A Study in Poetics* (Oxford, 1988), pp. 250–54; C. Prendergast, *The Order of Mimesis* (Cambridge, 1986), p. 220 ff.; A. Compagnon, *Le démon de la théorie* (Paris, 1998), pp. 139–40.

8. I elaborate on this point in *History, Rhetoric, and Proof*, The Menahem Stern Jerusalem Lectures (Hanover, N.H., 1999). I dwelt on the subject of narration and its implications in the conclusion of *Ecstasies: Deciphering the Witches' Sabbath* (New York, 1990).

9. C. Ginzburg, "Making Things Strange: The Prehistory of a Literary Device," *Representations* 56 (1996): 8–28, especially 19 ff.

10. Ginzburg, preface to *Clues, Myths, and the Historical Method*.

11. C. Ginzburg, *The Cheese and the Worms: The Cosmos of a Sixteenth-Century Miller* (Baltimore, 1980).

1. The Old World and the New Seen from Nowhere

1. Q. Skinner, "Sir Thomas More's *Utopia* and the Language of Renaissance Humanism," *The Languages of Political Theory in Early-Modern Europe*, ed. A. Pagden (Cambridge, 1987), pp. 123–157, especially pp. 123, 125, and 155. See also Skinner's cogent review of *Utopia*'s Yale edition in *Past and Present* 38 (1967): 153–168.

2. Only after having written these pages did I come across S. Rossi's excellent paper "Profilo dell'umanesimo enriciano: Erasmo e Thomas More," in *Ricerche sull'Umanesimo e sul Rinascimento in Inghilterra* (Milan, 1969), pp. 26–63, which has many insightful remarks on *festivitas*. See also S. Dresden, "Erasme, Rabelais et la 'festivitas' humaniste," in *Colloquia Erasmiana Turonensia*, vol. 1 (Paris, 1972), pp. 463–78 (brought to my attention by Ofer Nur).

3. C. S. Lewis, *English Literature in the Sixteenth Century Excluding Drama* (Oxford, 1954), p. 165 ff., especially p. 167.

4. See especially P. R. Allen, "*Utopia* and European Humanism: The Function of the Prefatory Letters and Verses," *Studies in the Renaissance* 10 (1963): 91–107.

5. P. S. Allen, *Opus Epistolarum Des. Erasmi Roterodami* (henceforth referred to as Allen) (Oxford, 1910), vol. 2, letters 461, 467, 474, 477, 481, 484, 487, 491, 499, 502, 508, 513, 524, 530, 534, and 537.

6. A detailed description has been provided by J. H. Lupton in *The Utopia of Sir Thomas More* (Oxford, 1895), p. lxiv ff.

7. "Superioribus hisce diebus ornatissime Buslidi, misit ad me Thomas ille Morus . . . Utopiam insulam, paucis adhuc mortalibus cognitam, sed dignam in primis quam ut plus quam Platonicam omneis velint cognoscere, praeser-

tim ab homine facundissimo sic expressam, sic depictam, sic oculis subiectam, ut quoties lego, aliquanto plus mihi videre videar, quam cum cum ipsum Raphaëlem Hythlodaeum (nam ei sermoni aeque interfui ac Morus ipse) sua verba sonantem audirem. . . . Attamen eadem haec quoties Mori penicillo depicta contemplor, sic afficior, ut mihi videar nonnunquam in ipsa versari Utopia" (*Utopia*, vol. 4 of *The Complete Works of St. Thomas More* [henceforth CW], ed. E. Surtz, S.J. and J. H. Hexter [New Haven, 1965], pp. 20–21). See also Jerome de Busleyden, *His Life and Writings*, ed. H. de Vocht, Humanistica Lovaniensia 9 (Turnhout, Belgium, 1950).

8. C. Ginzburg, "Montrer et citer," *Le Débat*, no. 56 (September–October 1989): 43–54.

9. CW 4:22: "Tetrastichum vernacula Utopiensium lingua scriptum, quod a Mori discessu, forte mihi ostendit Hythlodaeus apponendum curavi, praefixo eiusdem gentis alphabeto, tum adiectis ad margines aliquot annotatiunculis. Nam quod de insulae situ laborat Morus, ne id quidem omnino tacuit Raphaël, quanquam paucis admodum, ac velut obiter attigit, velut hoc alij servans loco. Atque id sane nescio quo modo casus quidam malus utrique nostrum invidit. Siquidem cum ea loqueretur Raphaël, adierat Morum e famulis quispiam, qui illi nescio quid diceret in aurem, ac mihi quidem tanto attentius auscultanti, comitum quispiam, clarius, ob frigus opinor, navigatione collectum, tussiens, dicentis voces aliquot intercepit. Verum non conquiescam, donec hanc quoque partem ad plenum cognovero, adeo ut non solum situm insulae, sed ipsam etiam poli sublationem sim tibi ad unguem redditurus, si modo incolumis est noster Hythlodaeus." I have made slight changes in the translation.

10. G. Genette, *Seuils* (Paris, 1967).

11. Philostratus the Elder, *Imagines*, trans. A. Fairbanks, The Loeb Classical Library (Cambridge, Mass., 1960), I, 22 [23]. See *Petrus Christus: Renaissance Master of Bruges* (catalog of the exhibition), ed. M. W. Ainsworth, with contributions by M. P. J. Martens (New York, 1994), pp. 93–95; A. Chastel, *Musca depicta* (Milan, 1984); E. Panofsky, *Early Netherlandish Painting* (Princeton, 1955), pp. 488–89 n. 5. See also J. B. Trapp, "Thomas More and the Visual Arts," in *Essays on the Renaissance and the Classical Tradition* (London, 1990), pp. 27–54. The comparison between More's passage and Petrus Christus has been inspired by S. Sandström, *Levels of Unreality* (Uppsala, 1963).

12. CW 4:40. The original of the last sentence reads "Nam ut maxime curabo, ne quid sit in libro falsi, ita si quid sit in ambiguo, potius mendacium dicam, quam mentiar, quod malim bonus esse quam prudens."

13. According to Aulus Gellius (*Noctes Atticae*, 11.11. 1–4), Publius Nigidius used to say, "There is a difference between telling a falsehood and lying. One who lies is not himself deceived, but tries to deceive another; he who tells a falsehood is himself deceived" (inter mendacium dicere et mentiri distat. Qui mentitur ipse non fallitur, alterum fallere conatur; qui mendacium dicit, ipse fallitur) (CW 4:292).

14. CW 4:252–253.

15. On the importance of hypothetical reasoning in More's work, see W. R. Davis, "Thomas More's *Utopia* as Fiction," *Centennial Review* 24 (1980): 249–68; and S. Greenblatt, "At the Table of the Great: More's Self-Fashioning and Self-Cancellation," in *Renaissance Self-Fashioning: From More to Shakespeare* (Chicago, 1984), pp. 11–73, especially pp. 32–33, an essay full of acute remarks, notwithstanding its acontextual approach.

16. CW 4:249–251: "Si res ut vera prodita est, video ibi quaedam subabsurda. Sin ficta tum in nonnullis exactum illud Mori iudicium requiro . . . si vulgi abuti ignoratione vellem litteratioribus saltem aliqua praefixissem vestigia quibus institutum nostrum facile pervestigarent. Itaque si nihil aliud ac nomina saltem principis, fluminis urbis insulae posuissem talia, quae peritiores admonere possent, insulam nusquam esse, urbem evanidam, sine aqua fluvium, sine populo esse principem, quod neque factu fuisset difficile et multo fuisset lepidius quam quod ego feci, qui nisi me fides coegisset hystoriae non sum tam stupidus ut barbaris illis uti nominibus et nihil significantibus, Utopiae, Anydri, Amauroti, Ademi voluissem." I have changed the translation of a few passages.

17. See CW 4:248 ff. E. Surtz, S.J., "More's *'Apologia pro Utopia sua,' " Modern Language Quarterly* 19 (1958): 319–24, focused on this letter but completely missed its meaning. More to the point is a passing remark by J. M. Levine in "Thomas More and the English Renaissance: History and Fiction in the *Utopia*," in *The Historical Imagination in Early Modern Britain: History, Rhetoric and Fiction, 1500–1800*, ed. D. R. Kelley and D. H. Sacks (Cambridge, 1997), pp. 69–82, especially p. 83.

Lupton, in his authoritative edition (Oxford, 1895) wrote that the additions to the second edition "were included in that of 1518, and are reprinted below" (*The Utopia*, p. lxviii), but he did not notice that More's second letter to Peter Giles had been omitted in the third and therefore failed to include it in his edition (see also p. ix). Lisa Jardine has suggested identifying More's second letter with the one Peter Giles holds in Metsys's portrait of him (*Erasmus: Man of Letters* [Princeton, 1993], pp. 40–41). But her hypothesis is not particularly compelling, since the small quarto volume on the table cannot be the octavo edition of *Utopia* published in Paris in 1517.

18. G. Vossius, *Opera* (Amsterdam, 1699), 4:340–341.

19. Ibid.

20. A. Prévost, *L'utopie* (Paris, 1978), pp. cii–ciii.

21. See *Meaning and Context: Quentin Skinner and His Critics*, ed. J. Tully (London, 1988).

22. T. S. Dorsch, "Sir Thomas More and Lucian: An Interpretation of *Utopia*," *Archiv für das Studium der neueren Sprachen und Literaturen* 203 (1966–67): 345–61, rightly argues, following C. S. Lewis's advice, that "the most profitable approach to *Utopia* may be by way of More's fondness for Lucian" (p. 347). But his conclusion that More invites the reader to reject Utopia's laws is certainly untenable: see D. Duncan, *Ben Jonson and the Lucianic Tradition*, Cambridge 1979, pp. 52–76, especially p. 69. On the same topic see also J. K. McConica, *English Humanists and Reformation Politics under Henry VIII and Edward VI*, Oxford 1965, p. 15; C. Robinson, *Lucian and His Influence in Europe*, London 1979, especially pp. 131–33.

23. See Thomas More, *Translations of Lucian*, in CW 3, ed. C. R. Thompson (New Haven, 1974), part 1, p. xxiv. See R. W. Gibson, *St. Thomas More: A Preliminary Bibliography of His Works and of Moreana to the Year 1750* (New Haven, 1961), which regrettably does not always quote the titles *in extenso*: Lucian's translation published in 1506, for instance, is listed merely as "Lucianus, *Opuscula*."

24. C. Dionisotti, *Machiavellerie* (Turin, 1980), p. 210 ff. Francesco Vettori's dismissive remark on More's *Utopia* in his "Sommario della istoria d'Italia," in *Scritti storici e politici*, ed. E. Niccolini (Bari 1972), p. 145, might preserve an echo of the author's conversations with Machiavelli.

25. L. Febvre, *Le problème de l'incroyance au XVIe siècle: La religion de Rabelais* (Paris, 1942, 1968), passim.

26. *The Correspondence of Erasmus*, trans. R. A. B. Mynors and D. F. S. Thomson (Toronto, 1975), 2:122. See Allen, letter 199, 1:430–31.

27. Allen, letter 193 (preface to *Gallus*, to Christopher Urswick), 1:424–26; More, letter to Thomas Ruthall, in *Translations of Lucian*, in CW 3, part 1, 2 ff. *Festivitas* became part of the standard definition of Lucian: Jakob Moltzer, the Heidelberg professor, in introducing Lucian's complete works in Latin—a volume that included both Erasmus's and More's translations—wrote: "Est etenim omnino author hic talis, ut eadem elegantia, eademque festivitatem reddi prorsus nequeat" (*Luciani Samosatensis opera, quae quidem extant, e Graeco sermone in Latinum, partim iam olim diversis authoribus, partim nunc per Jacobum Micyllum translata* [Lyon, 1549], preface). Moltzer's pseudonym, "Micyllus," refers to one of the characters in Lucian's dialogue *Gallus*.

28. D. Knox, *Ironia: Medieval and Renaissance Ideas on Irony* (Leiden, 1989), p. 98 ff.

29. Allen, letter 191 (to Richard Whitford, preface to Erasmus's Declamation in reply to Lucian's *Tyrannicida*), 1:422–23; letter 193, 1:425–26.

30. *The Correspondence*, 2:101. See Allen, letter 187, 1:416–17.

31. Allen, letter 461, 2:339.

32. *The Correspondence*, 2:291. See Allen, letter 293, 2:561–562. The translation of Lucianus's *Dialogi* was published by Josse Bade on June 1, 1514; see Ph. Renouard, *Imprimeurs et libraires parisiens du XVIe siècle*, #251. See Allen letter 261, 1:512–13, for Erasmus's dedication to William Warham, dated April 29, 1512. According to Allen, 1:561, "the long interval between the preface and the publication necessitat[ed] a new letter," but he might simply have changed the date of the previous one. Perhaps the translation of *Saturnalia* was the latest piece in the whole group.

33. Lucian, *Works*, vol. 6, trans. K. Kilburn, Loeb Classical Library (Cambridge, Mass., 1990), pp. 123–25. See also M. I. Finley, "Utopianism Ancient and Modern," in *The Critical Spirit: Essays in Honor of Herbert Marcuse*, ed. K. H. Wolff and B. Moore, Jr. (Boston, 1968), pp. 3–20, especially pp. 9–10.

34. CW 4:11–13. I made a slight change in the translation of the passage quoted above.

35. Lucian, *Works*, vol. 1, trans. A. M. Harmon, Loeb Classical Library (Cambridge, Mass., 1991), pp. 321–23.

36. CW 4:183.

37. *The Correspondence*, 2:116. See Allen, letter 193, 1:425–26: "Sic seria nugis, nugas seriis miscet; sic ridens vera dicit, vera dicendo ridet; sic hominum mores, affectus, studia quasi penicillo depingit, neque legenda, sed plane spectanda oculis exponit."

38. See C. R. Thompson, introduction to More, *Translations of Lucian*, in CW 3, part 1, pp. xxxv–xxxvi; and S. F. Bonner, *Roman Declamation in the Late Republic and Early Empire* (Liverpool, 1949). Ulrich von Hutten, in publishing Lorenzo Valla's tract on the alleged donation of Constantine, labeled it a *declamatio*, but see W. Setz, *Lorenzo Valla's Schrift gegen die Konstantinische Schenkung* (Tübingen, 1975), pp. 46–47.

39. C. Dornavius, *Amphitheatrum sapientiae ioco-seriae . . .* (Hanoviae, 1619; reprinted, Frankfurt am Main, 1670). On Dornavius's *Amphitheatrum* and mock encomia as "an inherently ironic genre," see a passing remark in Knox, *Ironia*, p. 93. See also A. Hauffen, "Zur Litteratur der ironischen Enkomien," *Vierteljahrschrift für Litteraturgeschichte* 6 (1893): 161–85; A. S. Pease, "Things Without Honor," *Classical Philology* 21 (1926): 27–42; Sister G. Thompson, "Erasmus and the Tradition of Paradox," *Studies in Philology* 61 (1964): 41–63; R. L. Colie, *Paradoxia Epidemica: The Renaissance Tradition of Paradox* (Princeton, 1966).

40. A. Warburg, "Pagan-Antique Prophecy in Words and Images in the Age of Luther," in *The Renewal of Pagan Antiquity* (Los Angeles, 1999), p. 617. See also R. Klibansky, E. Panofsky, and F. Saxl, *Saturn and Melancholy* (London, 1964), p. 134 n. 19; L. Bertelli, "L'utopia greca," in *Storia delle idee politiche, economiche e sociali*, ed. L. Firpo (Turin, 1982), pp. 463–581, especially pp. 521–22. On German prognostications in 1524, see P. Zambelli, "Fine del mondo o inizio della propaganda?" in *Scienze, credenze occulte, livelli di cultura* (Florence, 1982), pp. 291–368; *"Astrologi hallucinati": Stars and the End of the World in Luther's Time*, ed. P. Zambelli (Berlin, 1986). On the reworking of Lucian's writings in one of these prognostications, see A.-M. Lecoq, "D'après Pigghe, Nifo et Lucien: Le rhétoriqueur Jean Thénaud et le déluge à la cour de France," in *"Astrologi,"* pp. 215–37.

41. See S. Zavala, *Ideario de Vasco de Quiroga* (Mexico City, 1941); S. Zavala, *Sir Thomas More in New Spain* (London, 1955); F. B. Warren, "Don Vasco de Quiroga utopien," Festschrift for E. F. Rogers, *Moreana* 15–16 (1967): 385–94; and especially R. Dealy, *The Politics of an Erasmian Lawyer: Vasco de Quiroga* (Malibu, 1976).

42. C. Herrejón Peredo, ed., *Información en derecho del licenciado Quiroga sobre algunas pro-visiones del Real Consejo de Indias* (Mexico City, 1985), p. 200: "Este autor Tomás Moro fue gran griego y gran experto y de mucha autoritad, y tradujo algunas cosas de Luciano de griego en latín, donde, como dicho tengo, se ponen las leyes y ordenanzas y costumbres de aquella edad dorada y gentes sim-plecísimas y de oro della, según que parece y se colige por lo que en su república dice de éstos, y Luciano de aquéllos en sus *Saturniales*, y debiérale parecer a este varón prudentísimo, y con mucha cautela y razón, que para tal gente, tal arte y estado de república convenía y era menester, y que en sola ella y no en otra se podía conservar por las razones todas que dichas son." See M. Bataillon, "Erasme et le Nouveau Monde," in *Erasme et l'Espagne*, new ed. in 3 vols., text established by D. Devoto, ed. Ch. Amiel (Geneva, 1991), 3:469–504, especially pp. 488–89.

43. Peredo, *Información*, p. 188 ff., especially p. 197.

44. See J. A. Schumpeter, *History of Economic Analysis* (New York, 1954), p. 305.

45. C. Ginzburg, *Occhiacci di legno: Nove riflessioni sulla distanza* (Milan, 1998), pp. 40–81.

46. R. J. Schoeck, "A Nursery . . . ," in *Essential Articles for the Study of Thomas More*, ed. R. Sylvester and G. P. Marc'hadour (Hamden, Conn., 1977), p. 281 ff., especially p. 285 ff.

47. Greenblatt, "At the Table of the Great," pp. 22–23, 58.

48. J. H. Hexter, *More's "Utopia": The Biography of an Idea* (Princeton, 1952), pp. 18–21; idem, introduction to *Utopia*, CW 4:xviii–xx.

49. Lucian, *Works*, 1:357.

50. G. M. Logan, *The Meaning of More's "Utopia"* (Princeton, 1983), pp. 7 n. 6, IX.

51. See C. R. Thompson, *Translations of Lucian*, in CW 3, part 1, p. l n. 1.

52. This connection has been missed, if I am not mistaken, by most (if not all) scholars who have dealt with More's *Utopia*.

53. Lucian, "Philosophies for Sale," in *Works*, vol. trans. A. M. Harmon, Loeb Clas-sical Library (Cambridge, Mass., 1988), p. 450 ff.

2. Selfhood as Otherness

1. *The Journals and Papers of Gerard Manley Hopkins*, ed. H. House, completed by G. Storey (London, 1959), p. 84 ("an essay written for the Master of Balliol [?] 1865").

2. *Language* 42 (1966): 399–429, reprinted in R. Jakobson, *Poetica e poesia*, ed. R. Picchio (Turin, 1985), pp. 256–300.

3. Most recently by R. Helgerson, *Forms of Nationhood: The Elizabethan Writing of England* (Chicago, 1992), pp. 25–40. See also G. G. Smith, ed., *Elizabethan Critical Essays*, 2 vols. (Oxford, 1904). F. Zschech, *Die Kritik des Reims in England* (Berlin, 1917) basically depends on Smith.

4. London, 1589. See also L. V. Ryan, *Roger Ascham* (Stanford, 1963), as well as Ryan's edition of *The Schoolmaster* (Ithaca, 1967); and T. M. Greene, "Roger Ascham: The Perfect End of Shooting," *English Literary History* 36 (1969): 609–25.

5. For a comprehensive list, see M. A. Scott, *Elizabethan Translations from the Italian* (New York, 1916) (still very useful).

6. C. S. Lewis, *English Literature in the Sixteenth Century Excluding Drama* (Oxford, 1954), p. 281.

7. E. H. Gombrich, *The Ideas of Progress and Their Impact on Art* (New York, 1971), p. 10, quoting Aulus Gellius, *Noctes Atticae*, XIX, 8, 15. See E. R. Curtius, *European Literature and the Latin Middle Ages* (New York, 1953), pp. 247–72.

8. Here is an example of Figliucci's verse translation from Hesiod: "Chi per se stesso ben discorrendo risolve / Il meglio, a gli altri va sempre com'ottimo innanzi / Buono anco è quegli, ch'obedisce a i saggi ricordi. / Ma chi né 'ntende per sé, né 'ntende per altri, / Ben ch'oda, o pensi, del tutto disutile parmi" (F. Figliucci, *De la filosofia morale libri dieci, sopra li dieci libri de l'Ethica d'Aristotile* [Rome, 1551], p. 18).

9. G. G. Smith, *Elizabethan Critical Essays*, 1:153.

10. G. Fernandez Oviedo, *Historia general y natural de las Indias*, ed. J. Perez de Tudela Bueso, I (Madrid, 1959), l. V, ch. 1, pp. 112–116; see also José de Acosta, *Historia natural y moral de las Indias*, ed. B. G. Beddall (Valencia, 1977), l. VI, ch. 28, p. 447 (both mentioned in Smith, *Elizabethan Critical Essays*, 1:384.)

11. A. Grafton, *New Worlds, Ancient Texts* (Cambridge, Mass., 1992).

12. J. Amyot, *Les vies des hommes illustres Grecs et Romains, comparées l'une avec l'autre par Plutarque de Chaeronee, translatées de Grec en François, à Paris*, printed by Michel de Vascosan in 1554 (copy on vellum, previously owned by Mlle de La Vallière, Bibliothèque Nationale Paris): "Aux lecteurs: 'Je veux donques laisser à part l'excellence et la dignité de la chose en soy [l'histoire], veu que non seule-

ment elle est plus ancienne que toute autre espèce d'escripture qui onques ait esté au monde, mais aussi qu'elle a eu cours entre les hommes, avant que l'usage des lettres mesmes y fust, pource que lors les vivans laissoyent à leurs successeurs la mémoire des choses passées, en chansons qu'ils faisoyent apprendre par coeur de main à main à leurs enfans, ainsi que lon a pu voir de nostre temps par l'exemple de barbares habitans és terres neufves Occidentales, qui sans conserve d'aucunes lettres avoyent la cognoissance des choses advenues bien huit cent ans auparavant.'"

13. S. Fox Morzillo, *De historiae institutione: Dialogus* (Antwerp, 1557), p. 11r–12r. (The relevance of this passage was pointed out to me many years ago by Alessandro Taverna.)

14. Published "à Paris, de l'imprimerie de Michel de Vascosan, demeurant rue Sainct Jaques, 1557." The translator used only his initials, C. D. A.

15. [J. Wolf], *Artis historicae penus*, 2 vols. (Basel, 1579), 1:593–742. Bauduin's treatise was followed by Fox Morzillo's *De historiae institutione*. See D. R. Kelley, *Foundations of Modern Historical Scholarship: Language, Law, and History in the French Renaissance* (New York, 1970), pp. 116–148; M. Turchetti, *Concordia o tolleranza? François Bauduin (1520–1573) e i "moyenneurs"* (Geneva, 1984).

16. Ph. Sidney, *The Complete Works*, ed. A. Feuillerat (Cambridge, 1923[?]), 3:130–133, especially p. 131.

17. Bauduin, in [Wolf], *Artis historicae penus*, 1:665: "Posteaquam historia factum aliquod descripserit cum suis circumstantiis, etsi eam liberali custodia septam, vellem cingeret omnium literarum eruditus quidam chorus: tamen rhetores novos ad id, quod recitatum erit, exaggerandum non invitabo. Nam amplificationes atque excursiones ociosorum hominum, qui, ut poeta et pictores, quidlibet audendi atque fingendi potestatem sibi arrogant, non minus quam ineptas allegorias ineptorum concionatorum, praecidendas esse sentio." On Horace's dictum, see A. Chastel, "Le *Dictum Horatii quidlibet audendi potestas* et les artistes (XIIIe–XVIe siècles)," in *Fables formes figures* (Paris, 1978), 1:363–76.

18. M. Turchetti, *Concordia*, pp. 209–10 and passim.

19. Bauduin, in [Wolf], *Artis historicae penus*, 1:648–49: "Et quod Germanis (ut de aliis nunc non loquar) olim accidit, multis populis accidisse. Corn. Tacitus ait: 'veteres Germani ignorasse quidem secreta literarum, sed antiquis carminibus

usos esse, fuisseque hoc unum apud eos memoriae et annalium genus.' Unde et lib. II loquens de Arminio: 'Canitur (inquit) adhuc barbaras adhuc gentes, Graecorum annalibus ignotus.' Quid igitur tandem? Eginhardus, bonus profecto eius rei, quam dicere nunc volo, testis, de suo Carolo Magno: 'Barbara (inquit) et antiquissima carmina, quibus veterum regum actus et bel- lica canebantur, scripsit memoriaeque mandavit.' Recitabo alterum non minus nobile exemplum. In novis, hoc est, nuper repertis Indiae Occidental- is insulis, tam dicuntur esse homines illiterati, et literarum tamen, tanquam Deorum cultores: ut cum audirent nostros ibi Christianos alioqui absentes, sic inter sese per epistolas colloqui, ut alter alterum intelligat, epistolas illas clausas adorarint, in quibus dicebant inclusum esse aliquem divinum inter- nuncium genium. Illi (inquam) tam illiterati homines multorum saeculorum historiam suae gentis memoriamque conservarunt, partim quibusdam temere effectis symbolis, ut Aegyptii notis hieroglyphicis, partim suis can- tionibus, quas alii alios docent, et in suis choraeis cantillant, quales choros vocant areytos."

20. A. Momigliano, "Perizonius, Niebuhr and the Character of Early Roman Tradi- tion," *Journal of Roman Studies* (1957), reprinted in *Secondo contributo agli studi classici* (Rome, 1984), pp. 69–87). On p. 70 n. 6, Momigliano ascribes to Justus Lipsius the combination of Tacitus and Eginhardus, which in fact had been already suggested by Bauduin.

21. E. Benveniste, *Le vocabulaire des institutions indo-europénnes* (Paris, 1969), p. 92.

22. [Wolf], *Artis historicae penus*, 1:623: "Et nos erimus tam degeneres, ut ne audire quidem velimus patriae historiae carmen? Caeterum id intelligere non pos- sumus, nisi et eorum, qui barbari dicuntur, memoriam teneamus. Si Galli, vel Britanni, vel Germani, vel Hispani, vel Itali sumus, ut de nostris loqui pos- simus, necesse est nos Francorum, Anglorum, Saxonum, Gothorum, Longo- bardorum historiam non ignorare. Cumque nostri cum Saracenis et Turcis saepe congressi sint, ne nescire quidem licet Saracenicam et Turcicam."

23. Kelley, *Foundations of Modern Historical Scholarship*; N. Edelman, *Attitudes of Seven- teenth-Century France Toward the Middle Ages* (New York, 1946).

24. [G. Puttenham], *The Art of English Poesie* (London, 1589; reprint, Menston, Eng- land, 1968), p. 7.

25. [Puttenham], *The Art of English Poesie*, p. 251.

26. C. Ginzburg, "Montaigne, Cannibals, and Grottoes," *History and Anthropology* 6 (1993): 125–55, especially pp. 146–48.

27. [Puttenham,] *The Art of English Poesie*, pp. 209–10. See D. Hay, "Italy and Barbarian Europe," in *Italian Renaissance Studies: A Tribute to the Late Cecilia M. Ady*, ed. E. F. Jacob (London, 1960), pp. 48–68.

28. E. Norden, *La prosa d'arte antica*, trans. B. Heinemann Campana (Rome, 1988), 2:815 n. 2, 876 n. 90. But the whole appendix on the history of rhyme is fundamental. See also L. A. Muratori, *Antiquitates Italicae* (Mediolani, 1740), vol. 3, diss. 40: "De rythmica veterum poesi et origine Italicae poeseos," coll. 683–712: "the first systematic account" (Norden, *La prosa*, p. 815 n. 1).

29. [Puttenham], *The Art of English Poesie*, p. 11.

30. See my "Montaigne, Cannibals, and Grottoes." See also P. Ayrault, *Discours de la nature: Varieté et mutation des loix*, published as an introduction to F. Grimaudet, *Paraphrase du droict de retraict lignager, recueillie des coutumes de France* . . . (Paris, 1567), c.ar: "Les hommes vivent en tous païs, mais non pas de la mesme viande et nourriture: aussi n'a il lieu, ou ilz ne soyent regiz et policez par loix, constitutions et coustumes, mais non pas semblables et pareilles loix ou coustumes."

31. See J. Chapelain, *Opuscules critiques*, ed. A. C. Hunter (Paris, 1936), p. 222. See also the introduction to J. B. Fischer von Erlach, *Entwurf einer historischen Architectur in Abbildung unterschiedener berühmten Gebäude des Altertums und fremder Völker* (Leipzig, 1721): "Les dessinateurs y verront, que les goûts des nations ne difèrent pas moins dans l'architecture, que dans la manière de s'habiller ou d'aprêter les viandes, et en les comparant les unes aux autres, ils pouront en faire un choix judicieux. Enfin ils y reconnoîtront qu'à la verité l'usage peut authoriser certaines bisarreries dans l'art de bâtir, comme sont les ornaments à jour du Gothique; les voûtes d'ogives en tiers point, les tours d'Eglise, les ornements et les toits à l'Indienne, où la diversité des opinions est aussi peu sujète à la dispute, que celle des goûts." See my "Style as Inclusion, Style as Exclusion," in *Picturing Science, Producing Art*, ed. C. A. Jones and P. Galison (London, 1998), pp. 27–54, especially p. 32.

32. See the harsh comment of the editor of Sir Philip Sidney, George Puttenham, and William Webbe, *Documents Illustrating Elizabethan Poetry*, ed. L. Magnus (Lon-

don, 1906), p. 128 n. 7: "The argument in this chapter is not convincing. If rhyme is merely a savage device for mnemonic convenience in the absence of writing, comparable to the convenience of nakedness *versus* clothes, the defence of rhyme falls to the ground. Superior antiquity is not necessarily a superior art."

33. [Puttenham], *The Art of English Poesie*, p. 257.

34. M. H. Abrams, *The Mirror and the Lamp: Romantic Theory and the Critical Tradition* (Oxford, 1953; reprint, Oxford, 1974), pp. 273–74.

35. F. Yates, *Giordano Bruno and the Hermetic Tradition* (Chicago, 1964), pp. 275–90. Bruno's work was translated by L. Williams in 1887–89 as *The Heroic Enthusiasts*.

36. [Puttenham], *The Art of English Poesie*, pp. 218–49.

37. Smith, *Elizabethan Critical Essays*, 1:240.

38. See S. A. Tannenbaum, *Samuel Daniel: A Concise Bibliography* (New York, 1942); M. MacKisack, "Samuel Daniel as Historian," *Review of English Studies* 24 (1947): 226–43; C. Seronsy, *Samuel Daniel* (New York, 1967); P. Spriet, *Samuel Daniel (1563–1619): Sa vie—son oeuvre* (Paris, 1968); J. L. Harner, *Samuel Daniel and Michael Drayton: A Reference Guide* (Boston, 1980).

39. See *The Works of Thomas Campion*, ed. W. R. Davis (London, 1969), pp. 287–317; G. Saintsbury, *A History of English Criticism* (Edinburgh, 1911; reprint, Edinburgh, 1962), pp. 39 ff., 70 ff.; E. Lowbury, T. Salter, and A. Young, *Thomas Campion: Poet, Composer, Physician* (London, 1970), especially pp. 76–89; D. Attridge, *Well-weighed Syllables: Elizabethan Verse in Classical Metres* (Cambridge, 1974); and W. R. Davis, *Thomas Campion* (Boston, 1987), pp. 104–13.

40. S. Daniel, *A Panegyrike with a Defence of Ryme* [1603; reprint, Menston, England, 1969), cc. G6v. On the book of nature, see Curtius, *European Literature*, pp. 319–26.

41. Daniel, *A Panegyrike*: "The Grecians held all other nations barbarous but themselves, yet *Pirrhus* when he saw the well ordered marching of the Romanes, which made them see their presumptuous errour, could say it was no barbarous maner of proceeding" (cc. G6v–Hr). See J. I. M. Stewart, "Montaigne's *Essays* and *A Defence of Ryme*," *Review of English Studies* 9 (1933): 311–12. The relevance of this passage has been missed by recent interpreters: in the latest account of the Elizabethan debate on rhyme (Helgerson, *Forms of Nationhood*, pp. 25–40), Montaigne is not mentioned. See, on the contrary, Spriet, *Samuel Daniel*, passim.

42. In M. de Montaigne, *The Essayes or Morall, Politike and Millitarie Discourses . . . The First Booke* (London, 1603). Daniel's poem is addressed "To my deare brother and friend M. John Florio."

43. See J. Feit, *Shakspere and Montaigne: An Endeavour to Explain the Tendency of "Hamlet" from Allusions to Contemporary Works* (London, 1884), pp. 61–62.

44. See R. Romeo, *Le scoperte americane nella coscienza italiana del Cinquecento* (Naples, 1971).

45. C. Dionisotti, *Europe in Sixteenth-Century Italian Literature* (the Taylorian Lecture delivered February 11, 1971) (Oxford, 1971), pp. 18–19.

46. See F. A. Yates, *John Florio* (Cambridge, 1934), p. 89. On Florio's translation, see also F. O. Matthiessen, *Translation: An Elizabethan Art* (Cambridge, 1931), pp. 103–68.

47. S. Daniel, *Poems and a Defence of Ryme*, ed. A. C. Sprague (Chicago, 1930; reprint, Chicago, 1972), p. xxxv, recalls a passage from Daniel's *History* (iv, 213), on the "stately structures" erected in the twelfth century by Roger, bishop of Sarum, "of whose magnificence and spacious minde" they were "memorialls left in notes of stone."

48. See Saintsbury, *A History of English Criticism*, pp. 39 ff., 70 ff.

49. F. Braudel, *Les Temps du monde*, vol. 3 of *Civilisation matérielle, économie et capitalisme, XVe–XVIIIe siècles* (Paris, 1979), p. 302.

3. A Search for Origins

1. L. Sterne, *The Life and Opinions of Tristram Shandy Gentleman*, ed. G. Petrie, with an introduction by C. Hicks (Harmondsworth, 1984), pp. 453–55.

2. Ibid., p. 424.

3. V. Shklovsky, *Theory of Prose*, trans. B. Sher (Normal, Ill., 1990), pp. 147–170, especially p. 170.

4. Sterne, *Tristram Shandy*, p. 201. He could have added Montaigne to the list; see J. Lamb, "Sterne's Use of Montaigne," *Comparative Literature* 32 (1980): 1–41.

5. T. W. Jefferson, "Sterne and the Tradition of Learned Wit," *Essays in Criticism* 1 (1951), pp. 225–48; W. C. Booth, "The Self-Conscious Narrator in Comic Fiction Before *Tristram Shandy*," *PMLA* 67 (1952): 163–85; B. L. Greenberg, "Sterne and Chambers' Encyclopaedia," *Modern Language Notes* 49 (1954): 560–62.

6. L. Sterne, *Tristram Shandy*, pp. 137–39; see also pp. 123–24, for a reference to Hogarth's *Analysis of Beauty* (1753), whose motto, from Milton's *Paradise Lost* (book 9, ll. 516–18) refers to the snake's (Satan's) beauty. Kent's motto is mentioned by Walpole: see his *History of Modern Taste in Gardening*, introduction by J. D. Hunt (New York, 1995), p. 49; see also M. Jourdain, *The Work of William Kent* (London, 1948), pp. 20–24. Sterne was obviously familiar with the so-called ha-ha taken from fortifications: the ditch, replacing the walls surrounding the garden, which has been labeled Kent's "capital stroke" (see Jourdain, *The Work*, pp. 74–75, on Le Blond, *Gardening* (1712), trans. G. James (London, 1712); the general relevance of "ha-ha" has been aptly stressed by G. Carabelli, *On Hume and Eighteenth-Century Aesthetics: The Philosopher on a Swing*, G. Krakover Hall (New York, 1995), p. 91 ff.

7. See, as an introduction to this crucial topic, W. B. Piper, "Tristram Shandy's Digressive Artistry," *Studies in English Literature* 1, no. 3 (summer 1961): 65–76.

8. Sterne, *Tristram Shandy*, pp. 616–17. See also p. 617: "Sterne uses this latter concept [i.e., train of ideas] as the explanation for much of the eccentric behaviour and conversation of his characters, and as the basis for many of the dazzling transitions of time and space which takes place in the novel." See P. M. Briggs, "Locke's *Essay* and the Tentativeness of Tristram Shandy," *Studies in Philology* 82 (1985): 493–520 (which includes a bibliography). Cautionary notes have been struck by D. Maskell, "Locke and Sterne; or, Can Philosophy Influence Literature?" *Essays in Criticism* 23 (1973): 22–39; and W. G. Day, "Tristram Shandy: Locke May Not Be the Key," in V. G. Myer, *Laurence Sterne: Riddles and Mysteries* (London, 1984), pp. 75–83.

9. Sterne, *Tristram Shandy*, p. 39.

10. K. MacLean, *John Locke and English Literature of the Eighteenth Century* (New Haven, 1936), p. 17, quoting W. L. Cross, *Life and Times of Laurence Sterne* (New Haven, 1929), pp. 301–92, quoting D.-J. Garat, *Mémoires historiques sur le XVIIIème siècle, et sur M. Suard*, 2d. ed., 2 vols. (Paris, 1821), pp. 148–49. See also J.-Cl. David, "Un voyage en Suisse en 1784: Quatorze lettres inédites de Jean Baptiste Antoine Suard et de sa femme," *Studies on Voltaire and the Eighteenth Century* 292 (1991): 367–422.

11. D.-J. Garat, *Mémoires . . . .*, pp. 148–49: "Cette philosophie que ceux qui savent la reconnaître où elle est, et où elle dirige tout secrètement, retrouvent et sen-

tent dans toutes les pages, dans toutes les lignes, dans le choix de toutes les expressions; à cette philosophie trop religieuse pour vouloir expliquer le miracle de sensations, mais qui, avec ce miracle dont elle n'a pas la témérité de demander raison et compte à Dieu, développe tous les secrets de l'entendement, évite les erreurs, arrive aux vérités accessibles; philosophie sainte, sans laquelle il n'y aura jamais sur la terre ni vraie religion universelle, ni vraie morale, ni vraie puissance de l'homme sur la nature."

12. This point has been already made by B. McCrea, "Stories That Should Be True? Locke, Sterne, and *Tristram Shandy*," in *Approaches to Teaching Sterne's Tristram Shandy*, ed. M. New, (New York, 1989), pp. 94–100, especially p. 98.

13. Sterne, *Tristram Shandy*, pp. 202–3.

14. J. Traugott, *Tristram Shandy's World: Sterne's Philosophical Rhetoric* (Berkeley, 1954), pp. 30, 45, 40.

15. F. Doherty, "Bayle and *Tristram Shandy*: 'Stage-loads of chymical nostrums and peripatetic lumber,' " *Neophilologus* 58 (1974): 339–48, especially p. 339. Significantly, the article is not mentioned in *Approaches to Teaching Sterne's Tristram Shandy*, the survey published by the Modern Language Association of America mentioned in n. 12, above.

16. "Je ne sai ce que c'est de méditer regulièrement sur une chose: je prens le change fort aisément; je m'écarte très-souvent de mon sujet; je saute dans des lieux dont on auroit bien de la peine à deviner les chemins, et je suis fort propre à faire perdre patience à un Docteur qui veut de la méthode et de la regularité partout" (P. Bayle, *Oeuvres diverses* [1737], 3:9, quoted by R. Whelan, *The Anatomy of Superstition: A Study of the Historical Theory and Practice of Pierre Bayle* [Oxford, 1989], p. 185).

17. E. Cassirer, *Der Philosophie der Aufklärung*, 2d ed. (Tübingen, 1932), p. 269 ff. See M. Völkel, "Zur 'Text-Logik' im *Dictionnaire* von Pierre Bayle: Eine historisch-kritische Untersuchung des Artikels *Lipsius (Lipse, Juste)*," *Lias* 20 (1993): 193–226. See in general A. Grafton, *The Footnote: A Curious History* (Cambridge, Mass., 1997).

18. *Digestum Vetus* (Venice, 1488–90), c. b r.

19. Des Maizeaux, "The Life of Mr. Bayle," in P. Bayle, *The Dictionary Historical and Critical . . .* , trans. Des Maizeaux, 2d ed., 5 vols. (London, 1734–38), 1:lxxvi.

20. H. Kenner, *Flaubert, Joyce, and Beckett: The Stoic Comedians* (London, 1964).

21. Doherty, "Bayle and *Tristram Shandy*," p. 343. See Bayle, *The Dictionary*, entry "Vayer (Francis de la Mothe le)," remark "E," 5:422.

22. E. Labrousse, *Pierre Bayle* (La Haye, 1963), 1:150–51, 253.

23. Bayle, *The Dictionary*, 5:837–58.

24. Ibid., 5:842 (transl. Des Maizeaux). See Molière, *La critique de l'Ecole des Femmes*, in *Oeuvres*, ed. E. Despois (Paris, 1876), 3:325–26: "Uranie: 'Non, vraiment. Elle ne dit pas un mot qui de soi ne soit fort honnête; et si vous voulez entendre dessous quelque autre chose, c'est vous qui faites l'ordure, et non pas elle, puisqu'elle parle seulement d'un ruban qu'on lui a pris.' Climène: 'Ah! ruban tant qu'il vous plaira; mais ce *le*, ou elle s'arrête, n'est pas mis pour des prunes. Il vient sur ce *le* d'étranges pensées. Ce *le* scandalise furieusement; et, quoi que vous puissiez dire, vous ne sauriez défendre l'insolence de ce *le*.' Elise: 'Il est vrai, ma Cousine, je suis pour Madame contre ce *le*. Ce *le* est insolent au dernier point, et vous avez tort de défendre ce *le*.' Climène: 'Il a une obscenité qui n'est pas supportable.' " E. Auerbach's remark "Molière is never lewd" (*Mimesis: The Representation of Reality in Western Literature*, trans. W. R. Trask [Princeton, 1953], p. 399) sounds for once unconvincing.

25. Bayle, *The Dictionary*, 5:842, 842 n. 32.

26. Sterne, *Tristram Shandy*, pp. 450–51. See also Carabelli, *On Hume*, p. 143, who speaks of blank spaces and censorship, mentioning C. G. Coqueley de Chaussepierre, *Le roué vertueux* (1770) (which I have not seen). See also R. Alter, "Tristram Shandy and the Game of Love," *American Scholar* 37 (1968): 316–23.

27. Ibid., p. 609. See also Shklovsky, *Theory of Prose*, pp. 163 ff., on euphemisms and estrangement.

28. L. Sterne, *Works* (Dublin, 1774), 4:264 (*Sermon* 18, on Judges 12:1–3).

29. See E. H. Gombrich, *Art and Illusion* (London, 1960), pp. 181–202 on A. Cozens's well-known book *A New Method of Assisting the Invention in Drawing Original Composition of Landscape*, a later (1785) pictorial development of the interaction between artist and public.

30. See Sterne, *Tristram Shandy*, pp. 122–23: "It is about an hour and a half's tolerable good reading since my uncle Toby rung the bell, when Obadiah was ordered to saddle a horse, and go for Dr Slop, the man-midwife;—so that no one can say, with reason, that I have not allowed Obadiah time enough, po-

etically speaking, and considering the emergency too, both to go and come;—though, morally and truly speaking, the man, perhaps, has scarce had time to get on his boots.

"If the hypercritic will go upon this; and is resolved after all to take a pendulum, and measure the true distance betwixt the ringing of the bell, and the rap at the door;—and, after finding it to be no more than two minutes, thirteen seconds, and three fifths,—should take upon him to insult over me for such a breach in the unity, or rather probability, of time;—I would remind him, that the idea of duration and of its simple modes, is got merely from the train and succession of our ideas,—and is the true scholastic pendulum,—and by which, as a scholar, I will be tried in this matter—abjuring and detesting the jurisdiction of all other pendulums whatever."

31. Ibid., p. 286. See V. Shklovsky, *Theory of Prose*, pp. 154 ff.; J.-J. Mayoux, "Variations on the Time-sense in Tristram Shandy," in *The Winged Skull: Papers from the Laurence Sterne Bicentenary Conference*, ed. A. H. Cash and J. M. Stedmond (London, 1971), pp. 3–18, especially p. 14.

32. I. Watt, *The Rise of the Novel: Studies in Defoe, Richardson and Fielding* (London, 1967), p. 292, referring to J. Traugott, *Tristram Shandy's World*, and E. Tuveson, *The Imagination as a Means of Grace* (Berkeley, 1960).

33. Sterne, *Tristram Shandy*, p. 576. See also Bayle, *The Dictionary*, entry "Zeno of Elea," remark K, 5:618–19.

34. I. Watt, "The Comic Syntax of 'Tristram Shandy,' " in *Studies in Criticism and Aesthetics, 1660–1800: Essays in Honor of Samuel Holt Monk*, ed. H. Anderson and J. S. Shea (Minneapolis, 1967), pp. 315–31.

35. R. H. Popkin, "Bayle and Hume," in his *The High Road to Pyrrhonism*, ed. R. A. Watson and J. E. Force (San Diego, 1980), pp. 149–59.

36. See N. Kemp Smith, *The Philosophy of David Hume* (London, 1941), especially appendix C ("Bayle"), pp. 325–38. See also the recent survey by G. Paganini, "Hume et Bayle: Conjonction locale et immaterialité de l'âme," in *De l'Humanisme aux Lumières: Bayle et le protestantisme, Mélanges en l'honneur d'Elisabeth Labrousse* (Oxford, 1996), pp. 701–13.

37. Bayle, *The Dictionary*, entry "Pyrrho," remark B, 4:654.

38. See, for instance, Bayle, *The Dictionary*, "Explanation II: How what I have said

concerning the objections of the Manichees, ought to be considered,"
5:815–29.

39. D. Hume, *A Treatise of Human Nature* (London, 1739), ed. L. A. Selby-Bigge (Oxford, 1955), 3, 2, 5, pp. 524–25. See Carabelli, *On Hume*, p. 17, on the Eucharist.

40. Bayle, *The Dictionary*, entry "Pyrrho," remark B, 4:654. A recent analysis of the dialogue between the two abbots, remarkable for its lack of historical perspective, simply ignored Hume's reading of Bayle: T. M. Lennon, "Bayle's Anticipation of Popper," *Journal of the History of Ideas* (1997): 695–705.

41. Sterne, *Tristram Shandy*, p. 492, also quoted by R. Gorham-Davis, "Sterne and the Delineation of the Modern Novel," in *The Winged Skull: Papers from the Laurence Sterne Bicentenary Conference*, ed. A. H. Cash and J. M. Stedmond (London, 1971), pp. 21–41, especially p. 32.

42. Hume, *A Treatise*, I, 4, 6, p. 252.

43. Hume, *A Treatise*, I, 4, 6, p. 262.

44. Bayle, *The Dictionary*, entry "Nestorius," "remark A," 4:347. See Whelan, *The Anatomy*, p. 31 ff.

45. Sterne, *Tristram Shandy*, p. 108.

46. Ibid., p. 500; see also Watt, *The Rise of the Novel*, p. 291.

4. Tusitala and His Polish Reader

1. *The Works of Robert Louis Stevenson*, Swanston edition (London, 1912) (henceforth *The Works*), 18:414 ff.: *Letters to young people*: to miss B . . . (Vailima Plantation, Spring 1892), p. 418, signed "Tusitala (Tale-writer)"; next two letters signed "Tusitala"; idem, *The Letters* . . . , ed. B. A. Booth and E. Mehew (henceforth *Letters*) (New Haven, 1995), 7:300 n. 2415): May 1892 to Sidney Colvin, the natives call him "alii Tusitala," "The Chief Write-Information."

2. *Letters*, 7:95 n. 2307.

3. Ibid., 7:461 n. 2514, to Sidney Colvin, December 28(?), 1893, Vailima.

4. *The Works of Robert Louis Stevenson*, 17:274.

5. To Sidney Colvin, December 3, 1892, *Letters*, 7:436 n. 2496.

6. See, for example, R. L. Stevenson, "The Bottle Imp," in *The Strange Case of Dr. Jekyll and Mr. Hyde and Other Stories*, ed. C. Harman (London, 1996), pp. 225–50

7. *Grimmelshausens Werke in vier Bänden* (Weimar, 1964): *Trutz Simplex: Oder ausführ-*

liche und wunderseltsame Lebensbeschreibung der Erzbetrügerin und Landstörzerin Couräsche . . . , ch. 18, 3:84–90: see A. Ludwig, "Dahn, Fouqué, Stevenson," *Euphorion* 17 (1910): 613–24.

8. In vol. 2 of *The Acting National Drama* . . . , ed. B. Webster (London, 1838); see J. W. Beach, "The Sources of Stevenson's *Bottle Imp*," *Modern Language Notes* 25 (January 1910): 12–18. The erudite data have been conveniently reassembled in B. F. Kirtley, "The Devious Genealogy of the 'Bottle-Imp' Plot," *American Notes and Queries* 9 (January 1971): 67–70.

9. To W. E. Henley, April 1883, *Letters*, 4:97 n. 1083, note 4.

10. Quoted in Beach, "The Sources," p. 13.

11. P. Brooks, *The Melodramatic Imagination: Balzac, Henry James, Melodrama, and the Mode of Excess* (New Haven, 1976).

12. V. Propp, *Morphology of the Folk-tale* . . . (Austin, 1968). See F. Moretti, *Atlas of the European Novel, 1800–1900* (London, 1999), p. 109.

13. Beach, "The Sources," p. 14 n. 10.

14. G. Lukács, *Il marxismo e la critica letteraria* (Turin, 1964), p. 395.

15. Brooks, *The Melodramatic Imagination*, p. 86. See also A. Pieyre de Mandiargues, introduction to H. de Balzac, *La Peau de chagrin* (Paris, 1974), p. 13; and Brooks, *The Melodramatic Imagination*, pp. 14–15.

16. H. de Balzac, *The Wild Ass's Skin*, trans. H. J. Hunt (Harmondsworth, 1977), p. 45. The original reads: "Cette vision avait lieu dans Paris, sur le quai Voltaire, au dix-neuvième siècle, temps et lieux où la magie devait être impossible" (*La Peau de chagrin*, vol. 10 of *La Comédie humaine*, Bibliothèque de la Pléiade [Paris, 1979], p. 79).

17. Ibid., p. 45. The original reads: "La maison où le dieu de l'incredulité française avait expiré . . . agité par l'inexplicable pressentiment de quelque pouvoir étrange . . . cette émotion était semblable à celle que nous avons tous éprouvée devant Napoléon" (*La Peau de chagrin*, p. 79).

18. Ibid., p. 223. The original reads: "Quoi! . . . Dans un siècle de lumières où nous avons appris que les diamants sont les cristaux du carbone, à une époque où tout s'explique, où la police traduirait un nouveau Messie devant les tribunaux et soumettrait ses miracles à l'Académie des Sciences, dans un temps où nous ne croyons plus qu'aux paraphes des notaires, je croirais,

moi! à une espèce de *Mané, Thekel, Pharès?* . . . Allons voir les savants"] (*La Peau de chagrin*, p. 237).

19. Quoted by J. DeBois King, *Paratextuality in Balzac's La Peau de Chagrin (The Wild Ass's Skin)* (Lewiston, N.Y., 1992), p. 21.

20. Balzac, *La Comédie humaine*, 10, p. 1213 (introduction to *Etudes philosophiques*, 1834, signed by Félix Davin and reworked by Balzac). See F. Moretti, *Signs Taken for Wonders*, London, p. 293 n. 10: "Besides, the 'straight path'/'tortuous path' opposition is one of the main paradigms in Balzac's work."

21. Cited in Brooks, *The Melodramatic Imagination*, p. 118.

22. *Karl Marx: Interviews and Recollections*, ed. D. McLellan (London, 1981), p. 70.

23. I am echoing a famous remark by Baudelaire ("Théophile Gauthier," in *Oeuvres complètes*, ed. Cl. Pichois, Bibliothèque de la Pléiade, 2 [Paris, 1976], p. 120).

24. S. Petrey, "The Reality of Representation: Between Marx and Balzac," *Critical Inquiry* 14 (1988): 448–68.

25. K. Marx, *Capital*, trans. B. Fowkes (New York, 1977), 1:163–77. S. Weber, *Unwrapping Balzac: A Reading of La Peau de Chagrin* (Toronto, 1979), approaches this topic from a very different perspective.

26. To Charles Baxter, Edinburgh, March 28, 1872, *Letters* (New Haven, 1994), 1:219 ff. n. 96.

27. M. Proust, *Pastiches et mélanges* (Paris, 1948), pp. 11–87.

28. September 30, 1883, *Letters* (New Haven, 1994), 4:168–69 n. 1148.

29. F. Orlando, *Ricordo di Lampedusa* (Turin, 1996), pp. 45–47.

30. Stevenson, "The Bottle Imp," pp. 232, 235–36.

31. Balzac, *The Wild Ass's Skin*, p. 48.

32. *Popular Tales and Romances of the Northern Nations* (London, 1823), p. 107.

33. T. Roscoe, *The German Novelists*, translated from the originals, n.d., pp. 294–310.

34. B. Malinowski, *A Diary in the Strict Sense of the Term*, trans. N. Guterman (Stanford, 1989); *The Story of a Marriage: The Letters of Bronislaw Malinowski and Elsie Masson*, ed. H. Wayne, 2 vols. (London, 1995).

35. I. M. Lewis, *Man*, n.s., 3 (1968): 348–49.

36. Malinowski, *Diary*, p. 98.

37. B. Malinowski, "Kula: The Circulating Exchange of Valuables in the Archipelagoes of Eastern New Guinea," *Man* 20 (July 1920): 97–105.

38. R. J. Thornton, " 'Imagine yourself set down . . .': Mach, Frazer, Conrad, Malinowski and the Role of Imagination in Ethnography," *Anthropology Today* 1, no. 5 (1985): 7–14, especially p. 11.

39. Kula was referred to (albeit not mentioned by name) by Rev. Gilmour in the British New Guinea Annual Report for 1904–1905: see B. Malinowski, *Argonauts of the Western Pacific* (1922; reprint, New York, 1961), p. 500 n.

40. See R. Firth, ed., *Man and Culture: An Evaluation of the Work of Bronislaw Malinowski* (London, 1957), especially R. Firth, "The Place of Malinowski in the History of Economic Anthropology," pp. 209–27); J. P. Singh Uberoi, *Politics of the Kula Ring: An Analysis of the Findings of Bronislaw Malinowski* (Manchester, 1962); *The Ethnography of Malinowski: The Trobriand Islands 1915–1918*, ed. M. W. Young (London, 1979); J. W. Leach and E. R. Leach, eds., *The Kula: New Perspectives on Massim Exchange* (Cambridge, 1983); *Malinowski Between Two Worlds: The Polish Roots of an Anthropological Tradition*, ed. R. Ellen, E. Gellner, G. Kubica, and J. Mucha (Cambridge, 1988); and *The Early Writings of Bronislaw Malinowski*, ed. R. J. Thornton and P. Skalník, with a detailed introduction (Cambridge, 1993).

41. Malinowski, *Argonauts*, p. 477.

42. *The Story of a Marriage*, 1:48. See also ibid., 1:61, 63, which describe how Malinowski tried to collect evidence about the kula in Samarai and the neighboring island of Sariba.

43. Malinowski, *Argonauts*, pp. 83–84 (author's italics).

44. Malinowski, *Diary*, p. 114.

45. L. Fleck, *Genesis and Development of a Scientific Fact* (1935; reprint, Chicago, 1979).

46. *The Story of a Marriage*, 1:37. And then, a few days later (November 2, 1917): "Don't you think a (sea) voyage together would be lovely, Bronio? You know how R.L.S. used to cruise around the South Sea Islands in any old ship, and carry 'out his work all the while, and wring such a lot of romance and interest besides health out of his life" (p. 40).

47. Ibid., 1:75–76.

48. Malinowski, *Diary*, p. 199. See also *The Story of a Marriage*, 1:110, Oburaku, February 13, 1918: "In Gusaweta I read *The Secret Agent* by J[oseph] C[onrad] and I think that it is not only an inferior book but it has something loathsome about it." *Heart of Darkness*, M. W. Young has recently written, is "a somber sub-

text of Malinowski own diaries" (*Malinowski's Kiriwina: Fieldwork Photography, 1915–1918* [Chicago, 1998], p. 13).

49. *Vailima Letters: Being a Correspondence Addressed by Robert Louis Stevenson to Sydney Colvin, November 1890–October 1894* (New York, 1896), 1:112.

50. Malinowski, *Diary*, pp. 109–10, November 10, 1917: "Lecherous thoughts. . . . And so, for the future: E.R.M. is my fiancée, and more, she alone, no one else, exists for me; I must not read novels, unless I am sick or in a state of deep depression."

51. In ibid., p. 128, November 23, 1917, Malinowski speaks to Leonard Murray "about the importance of my work. . . . I tried to control myself and to remember that I worked with immortality in view and that paying attention to this crew simply banalizes my work."

52. See also ibid., p. 244, April 5, 1918: "Impressions from *kula* (once again feeling of ethnographic joy)."

53. Ibid., p. 234. See N. Guterman, introduction to ibid., p. xxi.

54. Malinowski, *Argonauts*, pp. 211–12.

55. E. Gellner, " 'Zeno of Cracow' or, 'Revolution at Nemi'; or, 'The Polish Revenge: A Drama in Three Acts,' " in *Malinowski Between Two Worlds: The Polish Roots of an Anthropological Tradition*, ed. R. Ellen et al. (Cambridge, 1988), pp. 164–94.

56. The scholar who came closest to this is A. K. Paluch, "The Polish Background to Malinowski's Work," *Man*, n.s., 16 (1981): 276–85. But see also some intriguing hints in Malinowski's letters to Elsie Masson (*The Story of a Marriage*, 1:59, 65, 121–22.

57. Malinowski, *Diary*, p. 235 (italics in original).

58. P. Skalník, "Bronislaw Kasper Malinowski and Stanislaw Ignacy Witkiewicz: Science Versus Art in the Conceptualization of Culture," in *Fieldwork and Footnotes: Studies in the History of European Anthropology*, ed. H. F. Vermeulen and A. A. Alvarez Roldán (London, 1995), pp. 129–42, notwithstanding his rather dismissive attitude toward Malinowski, raises some important questions.

59. E. Leach, "The Kula: An Alternative View," in *The Kula: New Perspectives on Massim Exchange*, ed. J. W. Leach and E. Leach (Cambridge, 1983), pp. 529–38, especially pp. 534, 536.

60. See M. Mauss, *Oeuvres*, ed. V. Karady (Paris, 1968–69), "Les origines de la notion

de monnaie" (1914), 2:106–12, 114–15; "L'extension du *potlatch* en Mélanesie" (1920), 3:29–34; "Une forme ancienne de contrat chez les Thraces" (1920), 3:35–43; "L'obligation à rendre les présents" (1923), 3:44–45; "Gift, gift" (1924), 3:46–51; "Sur un texte de Posidonius: Le suicide, contre-prestation suprème" (1925), 3:52–57; and idem, "Essai sur le don" (1925), in *Sociologie et Anthropologie* (Paris, 1950), pp. 145–279.

Index